Starting Skills in English

Listening and Speaking
Part B

Teacher's Book

Terry Phillips & Anna Phillips

Garnet
EDUCATION

Published by
Garnet Publishing Ltd.
8 Southern Court
South Street
Reading RG1 4QS, UK

This edition first published 2006

ISBN 1 85964 812 6

British Library Cataloguing-in-Publication Data
A catalogue record for this book is available from
the British Library.

Production

Project manager:	Francesca Pinagli
Editorial team:	Rod Webb, Maggie MacIntyre
Art director:	David Rose
Design:	Mike Hinks
Typesetting:	Samantha Barden
Illustration:	Doug Nash, Karen Rose
	Beehive Illustration: (Colin Brown /
	Janos Jantner / Martin Sanders /
	Laszlo Veres)
Photography:	Banana Stock, Corbis, Digital Vision,
	Flat Earth, Image Source,
	Ingram Publishing, Photodisc, Stockbyte

Garnet Publishing wishes to thank the following for their
assistance in the piloting of this project:
David Anderson, Kaye Anderson, Alec Benson, Terry Boucher,
William Davis, Jeanette Drissi, Patrick Flavin, Bruce Gunn,
Marion King, Leslie Kirkham, Nicholas Lake,
Mairead Lyons-Hackett, Peter Newbery, Barbara Mary Rowell,
Roland Steinwand, Evan Sullivan, Yusuf Suluh, Kevin Watson,
Debra Wedl, John Wells and teachers and administrators from
the Higher Colleges of Technology in the UAE.

Special thanks go to Nicola Marsden and Hinemoa Xhori.

Every effort has been made to trace the copyright holders and
we apologize in advance for any unintentional omissions. We
will be happy to insert the appropriate acknowledgements in
any subsequent editions.

Audio production: Chris Dalby, YellowPark

Printed and bound
in Lebanon by International Press

Starting Skills in
English
Listening and Speaking
Part B

Contents

Book Map

Listening (Lessons 1 and 2)	Speaking (Lessons 3 and 4)
Theme 1 – Education	
• identifying multi-syllable words from the strong sound • predicting the next subject • predicting the next word or phrase	• talking about likes and dislikes (1) • talking about quantity • comparing two things
Theme 2 – Daily Life	
• guessing spelling	• talking about regular events: frequency adverbs, *sometimes* • asking about regular events: *usually, ever, often*
Theme 3 – Work and Business	
• end focus • guessing meanings	• asking about jobs
Theme 4 – Science and Nature	
• understanding the value of *and, but, or*	• asking about the weather • talking about the weather • starting a conversation (1): leaving words out
Theme 5 – The Physical World	
• guessing pronunciation • using drawings and diagrams	• using *ago* • comparing notes: names and numbers

Listening (Lessons 1 and 2)	Speaking (Lessons 3 and 4)
Theme 6 – Culture and Civilization	
• identifying questions: asking for *Yes/No* answers/information	• making and answering questions
Theme 7 – They Made Our World	
• using the correct short form • predicting the structure of a talk • listening and reacting: alternatives – *Which is the best way?*	• improving your pronunciation • stressing long words • starting a conversation (2): by talking about travel
Theme 8 – Art and Literature	
• examples and lists	• talking about possibilities: *I think; perhaps; may be; probably*
Theme 9 – Sports and Leisure	
• recognizing change of subject: signpost language	• talking about likes and dislikes (2): *I like; My favourite; I hate; It makes me; I find it*
Theme 10 – Nutrition and Health	
• guessing pronunciation of vowels: recognizing similar patterns	• talking about containers (1): with a liquid – *a bottle of milk* • talking about containers (2): without a liquid – *a milk bottle* • *How much?* or *How many?*

INTRODUCTION

Why is *Starting Skills in English* different?

Starting Skills in English is designed exclusively for teenage and young adult false beginners. Many courses claim to be suitable for this target group, but do not consider the real profile of their target students.

- False beginners are **not** true beginners. They are people with a great deal of passive knowledge, especially of vocabulary, in whom later learning has driven out earlier basic points. *Starting Skills in English* systematizes this previous learning so it can become genuinely useful.

- False beginners are **not** effective language learners who have simply forgotten previous learning. Therefore, they will not benefit, in the main, from a revision course with a very fast syllabus progression. They need a course which lock-steps them through each point, to ensure that they understand it before moving on.

- *Starting Skills in English* takes students step by step through the basic points they should have learnt before, and demonstrates the communicative value of lexical, grammatical, orthographic and phonological points.

- False beginners, in many cases, are **not** read-write learners. They have struggled with the text-heavy materials in many school coursebooks. They may be visual learners, who need colour and pictures, or aural learners, who need sounds and repetition. They may even be kinaesthetic learners who need to touch things and move them around to make sense of them. *Starting Skills in English* recognizes different learning styles and gives students different ways of learning the same information.

- False beginners, in many cases, are **not** inductive learners. They have struggled to learn with the methodology of example to rule. They need to be given the opportunity to learn deductively as well, from rule – or perhaps we should say, pattern – to example. *Starting Skills in English* often gives students two routes – an inductive and a deductive way – with the use of overt *Skills Check* boxes for the deductive learner, and activities for the inductive learner.

- False beginners, in the main, have no desire to go 'right back to the beginning'. They may have low motivation to study English anyway, given their history of failure, but they will certainly not be motivated by things that even they find too easy or, at least, too familiar. *Starting Skills in English* aims to teach old points in a new way.

- As mentioned before, false beginners have, to some extent, failed previous learning. They have sat in classes for, perhaps, nine years, but they are still not able to pass a formal test of English at more than beginner level. This means they need to be convinced that they can succeed this time. *Starting Skills in English* aims to give success right from the start, with materials which are interesting and challenging for students, but within their grasp.

- False beginners in a class are **not** an homogenous group. For any given item of beginner-/elementary-level vocabulary or grammar, there will be someone in the group who knows the item and many others who do not. But the 'knower' will change from item to item. *Starting Skills in English* acknowledges previous successful learning and, at the same time, enables the teacher to see which students are struggling on a particular point so he/she can direct those students to the additional remedial work provided.

- False beginners can do very little with the language, even in areas where they have some knowledge. In other words, they have some competence but few or no specific performance skills in listening, speaking, reading or writing, which they will need for further study in English. *Starting Skills in English* introduces students to key points in the four skills.

What is the structure of *Starting Skills in English*?

Starting Skills in English is divided into two parts, A and B. Students can enter the course at A or B level. Each part provides at least 150 hours' tuition. The whole course, therefore, provides at least 300 hours' tuition.

There are three books in each part.
1 *Listening and Speaking*
2 *Reading and Writing*
3 *Vocabulary and Grammar*
It is assumed that most users of the course will teach the books in this order, although it is not essential. The majority of the material in the third book, *Vocabulary and Grammar*, could be set as self-study. The book is also linked to exercises on the dedicated *Starting Skills in English* website.

Each of the three books contains ten themes, based on the *Encyclopaedia Britannica* organization of human knowledge. This means that students learn useful, transferable content as well as useful transferable vocabulary and skills as they work through the course. *Starting Skills in English* does not assume that graduates from the course are going to become world travellers, using English as a lingua franca. Instead, it assumes they are going on to further study in English. Therefore, the themes covered build knowledge and skills which will assist in further English-medium study.

The ten themes are:
1 Education
2 Daily Life
3 Work and Business
4 Science and Nature
5 The Physical World
6 Culture and Civilization
7 They Made Our World
8 Art and Literature
9 Sports and Leisure
10 Nutrition and Health

Work within each theme is, therefore, constrained by a lexical set. This means that students gain in confidence in using a limited set of lexical items as they work through the theme, rather than constantly having to cope with new words which happen to appear in presentation texts.

Starting Skills in English recognizes that there is more to knowing a word than knowing its base meaning, and so by the end of each theme, students should be confident in using words in written or spoken form, and proficient at recognizing the word in both forms. They will often also know some common collocations of words in a theme and important grammatical points about words, such as plural formation.

What is the approach of *Starting Skills in English*?

Starting Skills in English adopts a recurrent structure within each theme. This is broadly a test–teach–test approach, which appears to be the best to accommodate all the needs of false beginners as previously detailed. In other words, students are first tested, informally, on the English they know in a particular area. There is then a range of teaching activities to ensure full competence in that area, then a final test, again informal, of the same points. It is worth pointing out that students may not notice the informal testing, since it is not flagged as a test except in Grammar. This is not a problem, since the main aim is to show teachers what students know/do not know, although it can also be motivating for students to realize that they need to learn particular items from a lexical set or a particular skill or grammar point.

The course is organized into themes. The same themes are used across the three books in Part B. Within each theme, there are four lessons.

Listening and Speaking and Reading and Writing

In each theme, **Lesson 1** is a test or deep-end strategy lesson on the receptive skills, listening or reading, in a particular theme area. Hopefully, students will get most items right in this lesson, thus confirming their false beginner (rather than true beginner) status. However, teachers are encouraged to make a note of students who get specific items wrong and to try to ensure that, by the end of Lesson 2, they are getting those items right.

Lesson 2 highlights and does remedial work on the receptive skill points in Lesson 1. In this lesson, there is also some productive work, in speaking or writing, of words and sentences that have been highlighted to date.

Lesson 3 is a test or deep-end strategy lesson on the related productive skill, speaking or writing, in a particular theme area. The purpose is the same as Lesson 1 – to motivate students and highlight points for remedial work. Once again, teachers are encouraged to make a note of students who get specific items wrong and try to ensure by the end of Lesson 4 they are getting that item right.

Lesson 4 highlights and does remedial work on the speaking or writing points in Lesson 3.

Note that this pattern becomes clearer as the course proceeds.

Vocabulary and Grammar

As with the other two books, **Lesson 1** is a test or deep-end strategy lesson on vocabulary in a particular theme area. Teachers are encouraged to make a note of students who get specific items wrong and follow one or more of these courses of action:

a   work with them individually during the lesson
b   work with small groups of students having the same problem during the lesson
c   refer students to remedial vocabulary work on the website.

Whatever action is taken, students should be retested afterwards to demonstrate that they have made progress.

In many lessons in Part B, there is one or more exercise in each theme on numbers, in addition to thematically-linked work. *Starting Skills in English* believes that proficiency with using numbers in speech and in writing is central to English-medium study and therefore devotes a considerable amount of time to this point, dealing with it systematically.

Lesson 2 covers more ground using a test/deep-end strategy. In many cases, there is a lexical grammar issue to be dealt with, such as modifying nouns. In this lesson, Skills Checks highlight points for specific learning.

Lesson 3 is a test or deep-end strategy lesson on grammar in a particular area. The purpose is the same as Lesson 1. Teachers are encouraged to note students who get specific items wrong. On this occasion, however, the remedial work is directly provided in Lesson 4. Students should therefore be tested again after they have completed this lesson to see if they have improved on weak items. There is often a text-to-note, note-to-text writing activity, with a strong grammatical focus.

Lesson 4 highlights and does remedial work on the grammar points in Lesson 3. If students are still struggling with these grammar points after the lesson, they should be referred to the website/CD for further remedial work.

Key activities

Vocabulary learning in general

Starting Skills in English believes that the key to good language learning is the acquisition of a broad, useful, transferable vocabulary. As mentioned before, vocabulary learning is not just about meaning. It is also about form in speech and writing, and about collocation and usage.

Starting Skills in English looks at a lexical set in each theme in each of the four skills in turn. Firstly, students are taught to hear the set of words, in isolation and in context. They are then given the opportunity to produce the same set of words in speech, in isolation and context. Then the same set of words is flashed at them, to improve the ability to recognize the word in written form at high speed. The words are then included in a variety of texts for recognition in context. Finally, students are given the opportunity to prove their ability to produce the same set of words in writing, with the correct spelling and usage.

Listening

Listen and point

This may look like a primary-level activity, but it is the best way to prove ability to relate objects and action verbs to the sound of the words, in isolation and the stream of speech, without having to engage in any other linguistic activity, e.g., speaking or writing. It greatly aids the aural learner and, because there is a physical element, may assist the kinaesthetic learner.

Listen and do

This TPR (Total Physical Response) activity may also look like a primary-level activity, but it is the best way to prove ability to relate spoken language to its communicative purpose without a linguistic output. It greatly aids the kinaesthetic learner.

Listen and tick the next word

A key listening skill is the ability to predict the next word. It is part of the hypothesis checking of active listening. We can only cope with the speed of incoming data in the stream of speech if we have to some extent predicted the content.

Listen and draw

This is another way of checking understanding without a linguistic output.

Skills Checks – hearing specific phonemes

How can a student recognize a word in the stream of speech if he/she cannot recognize the phonemes it contains? *Starting Skills in English* presents discrete phonemes, then phonemes in contrast, and checks the students' ability to hear, then discriminate.

Skills Checks – listening skills

Students are taught to listen for important words – a key skill.

Speaking

Look and name

This is the converse of *Listen and point*. At this point, the teacher can focus on ensuring that students can correctly name depicted items and make a reasonable approximation of the pronunciation.

Listen and look

Although this may appear to be a listening activity, it is actually an essential precursor to speaking. Students are usually given the opportunity to hear a conversation before reading it. This greatly helps aural learners, and ensures for all learners that there is an aural trace of sounds in their brain, which they can recover to help with their own pronunciation.

Work in pairs – information gap

Activities often involve an information gap – one student has information and the other has to close the gap.

Work in pairs – role play

Students are given the opportunity to practise transactional conversations which they have previously heard. This assists aural learners.

Work in pairs – talk about yourself

Students are given the opportunity to talk about themselves, using the patterns they have practised in a preceding role play.

Talk about yourself

This is often a development from *Work in pairs – talk about yourself*. Students are taught to take the individual sentences from the pairwork and turn them into a connected text for an oral presentation.

Ask and answer

This activity often contains dessicated sentences, i.e., sentences which only retain the function words. This kind of exercise probably mimics the production of sentences in the human brain. It is likely that we retrieve the content words first, then the function words which carry them in a given sentence.

Rebus conversations

A rebus is a picture which prompts a word or a sentence. It is a child's puzzle, but it is used in *Starting Skills in English* because it mimics real-world language production. We store meanings above linguistic level, then translate them into words. Thus, a picture of a map of England plus a question mark can prompt the question *Are you from England?*

This probably assists all learners, but especially visual learners.

Skills Checks – saying specific phonemes

Starting Skills in English presents discrete phonemes for accurate production, then phonemes in contrast, and checks the students' ability to say and/or discriminate. These Skills Checks often point out common sound-sight relationships, e.g., *ow* may be /əʊ/ or /ə/.

Reading

The texts

The majority of texts in *Starting Skills in English* are simulated authentic – in other words, they are pieces of written English that a student might actually encounter in their daily life or might have to read for their studies. The principal activities based on those texts are real-world – in other words, things that a person might really have to do while reading or after reading such a text. In addition, there are often analytical tasks which help students to recognize key points about the form or organization of information in the text, which will help them to read similar texts in the future.

Look and read

The teacher flashes words from the lexical set for students to recognize in written form. Response is in speech and one could argue that this is wrong as it requires a linguistic response. However, by this point, students have had the opportunity to produce the target words in speech on many occasions, so spoken response should, on the one hand, not be a challenge, and on the other, should provide a good revision of oral production.

Skills Checks – reading skills

Students are taken step by step through key reading skills, including basic points related to the decoding of written text.

Find and circle / underline / box

Students are required to annotate written text to show they can correctly identify key features of punctuation and recognize key parts of speech – noun, verb and adjective. This understanding of parts of speech is fundamental to being able to guess the meaning of a new word in context. If you do not know what part of speech it is, it will be very hard to guess the meaning.

Right or wrong?

Reading is made communicative from the very beginning. Students are asked to look at visual prompts and recognize whether sentences correctly describe what they see.

Writing

The tasks

The majority of writing tasks involve the production of real-world texts – in other words, pieces of connected prose that students might have to do as part of their English studies at a later date, rather than simply sentence-level manipulation of grammatical points.

Crosswords

These are an excellent way of checking a student's ability to name real items or recognize what is missing from a sentence, and produce the word with correct spelling. They are particularly useful for learners with a high tolerance of ambiguity.

Tick the correct sentences

Writing is made communicative from the very beginning. Students are asked to look at visual prompts and choose the correct sentence to describe what they see.

Read and complete

This usually involves the identification of the missing vowel because, in English, consonants are largely phonemic (sound = sight), whereas vowels are not. If students write the correct vowels in a word, the chances are the word will be correctly spelt.

Number the boxes in order

English is a syntagmatic language – in other words, meaning is largely carried by the order of words rather than by paradigms which indicate case or gender. Therefore, students need constant practice in putting words in an acceptable 'English' order. In *Starting Skills in English*, most sentences are based on the S V (C) (O) (A) pattern.

Skills Checks – spelling

These checks teach common patterns of sound-sight.

Skills Checks – writing skills

This is sometimes the converse of the Reading Skills Checks. For instance, students are asked to identify the capitalized words in Reading, then to add the capitals in the related Writing section. At other times, the Writing Skills Checks cover points which are not important to the reader, but vital to the writer. In particular, many of these checks cover points of grammaticized lexis such as the use of determiners with different kinds of nouns.

Vocabulary

General

It is assumed that students come to the lessons in a particular theme having studied the lexical set in speech and writing in the other two books. Therefore, there is a combination of listening (to the teacher), speaking, reading and writing in these lessons.

Number work

As mentioned before, there are many exercises on numbers. By the end of this course, students should be fully proficient with the complexities of this important, and often under-practised, issue.

Alphabet work

Students who come from a language with a different alphabet often struggle for years to recognize key features of English orthography and to reproduce them in their own writing. These exercises take such students step by step through these vital features.

Wordsearch

This is an excellent way to check a student's ability to pick out word shapes. It is well known now that good readers recognize words from their complete pattern rather than by decoding individual letters and then assembling them.

Collocation

A key point about words – 'we know them by the company they keep'. (Fries)

Synonymy, Antonym, Hyponymy, Hypernymy/Superordination

These are key points about semantic relationships between words, vital for lexical cohesion work later in their learning. For example, students must recognize that a *car* is a *vehicle*, otherwise they may not understand that the writer is referring to the same item even though he/she uses the two different words.

Grammar

Tests

These are diagnostic tests. Each item relates to one of the sentence or phrase patterns points in Lesson 4. Students and teacher alike can see points of difficulty at a glance.

Parallel production

Many themes contain this kind of task, where students are asked to use a model text to create a text of a similar nature about a different subject, or where information is transferred from, e.g., table to text, and back again.

Sentence and phrase patterns

English is an S V (C) (O) (A) language. Students need to gain a firm grasp of this concept and to understand what can fit into each of the categories. The sentence and phrase patterns in this section build into an invaluable compendium of this basic structure, which should ensure that students are confident to build from this to compound and complex sentences in later courses.

Colour coding is used in these sentence patterns. This greatly assists all students to match function and form in the pattern but is, of course, of especial value to the visual learner.

General note

By the end of this theme, students should be able to hear and identify, in isolation and in context, the following words linked with education. They should also be able to say them with reasonable pronunciation, especially stress in multi-syllable words, and use them in simple S V (O) (C) sentences with time phrases.

college	learn	secondary
explain	Mathematics (Maths)	spell
Geography	primary	study
History	Religious Studies	teach
IT	Science	university

Lesson 1: Listening

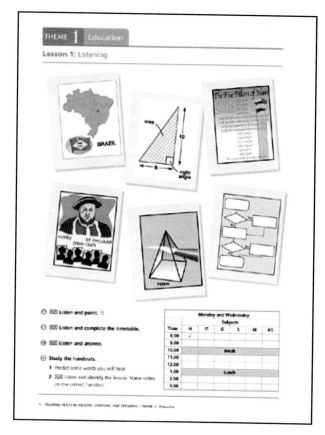

Introduction

Students may already be familiar with the following words from this lexical set:

answer	desk	question	teacher
ask	end	read	test
begin	listen	right	write
board	pen	speak	wrong
chair	pencil	student	

If you are in any doubt, check that all the students can identify and produce these words in isolation.

1 Say sentences containing each 'concrete' item and get them to point to or hold up the item in question.

2 Say one item from a pair and get students to say the converse, e.g., *read/write*. When you have gone through the words once, repeat at high speed.

Then put some or all of the words into sentence context. Use Total Physical Response (TPR) where possible, e.g., *Look at the board. Pick up your pencil.*

Ask questions for non-concrete items or actions, e.g., *Are you a student? What's the name of your teacher?*, etc.

Exercise A

Refer students to the illustrations. Ask them what they can see. Elicit any vocabulary items they know, but do not insist on other students saying or understanding the words.

Explain that they are going to hear some school subjects. They must point to the correct handout. Go through the first word (*Mathematics*) as an example. Make sure all the students are pointing to the handout with a triangle. Say or play the tape. Watch the students and try to identify any student who is not correctly associating the spoken word with the handout.

Tapescript

Presenter:	Theme 1 Education
	Lesson 1
	A Listen and point.
Voice:	Mathematics
	Science
	History
	Religious Studies
	Geography
	IT
Voices:	What time's Religious Studies?
	We're doing the 16th century in History at the moment.
	Where's my Geography book?
	Where's the IT lesson this afternoon?
	Do we have Mathematics today?
	What did we do in Science last lesson?

You can go through this activity several times, speeding up and saying words and sentences in a different order.

Language and culture note

This is a listening lesson, so the point may not arise, but we normally capitalize school subjects. Remember to use a capital letter if you write any of these words on the board.

Exercise B

Refer students to the timetable. Ask them what the abbreviations mean. They should be able to remember the names of the subjects. Get students to say the times, too. Do not worry too much about stress within words at the moment, but check that students are pronouncing the vowels correctly.

Ask some checking questions, e.g., *What time is the first lesson? What time is the last lesson? When is lunch? How long is each lesson?* Check or teach the words *break* and *lunch*.

Tell students they are going to hear information about the timetable. Ask *What time is History?* to show how students must mark the timetable with ticks.

Set for individual work and pairwork checking. Play the tape. Feed back, ideally onto an OHT of the timetable.

Answers

Monday and Wednesday						
	Subjects					
Time	H	IT	G	S	M	RS
8.00	✓					
9.00			✓			
10.00	Break					
11.00					✓	
12.00		✓				
1.00	Lunch					
2.00						✓
3.00				✓		

Tapescript

Presenter: B Listen and complete the timetable.

Voice: OK. I'm going to go through your timetable for this semester. You have six subjects each day: History, IT, Geography, Science, Maths and Religious Studies. But you don't have the subjects at the same time every day. So let's look first at Monday and Wednesday. You have History first, at eight o'clock. Next, you have Geography at nine. You have a break at ten. The next lesson begins at eleven, and that's Mathematics. After Maths, you have IT. Lunch is at one o'clock, then in the afternoon you start at two with Religious Studies. What's next? Oh yes, finally at three o'clock you have History. No, that's wrong. You have History in the morning. Science! You have Science at three.

Language and culture note

Mathematics is often abbreviated to *Maths* in British English, or *Math* in American English. *Information Technology* is almost always called *IT* or *ICT* (*C = Communications*). *Religious Studies* is often abbreviated to *RS*, but *RK*, *RI* and *RE* (*Knowledge / Instruction / Education*) are also used.

Exercise C

Set for whole-class work. Ask questions about the timetable, or play the tape. Make a note of students who are having difficulty understanding the questions.

Repeat, with or without the tape, but this time do not let students shout out the answers. Nominate a student after a pause. Do not insist on long answers as the aim is comprehension of the questions in spoken form.

Answers

Model answers:

When do we have Geography?	*At 9.00.*
What time's IT?	*At 12.00.*
Do we have Science in the afternoon?	*Yes, at 3.00.*
How many subjects do we have in the morning?	*Three.*
How long is lunch?	*One hour.*
Do we have Maths in the morning or the afternoon?	*The morning, at 11.00.*
Is History the first lesson on Monday?	*Yes, it is.*
Is Religious Studies the last lesson?	*No, it isn't.* *(It's Science.)*

Tapescript

Presenter: C Listen and answer.

Voice: When do we have Geography?
What time's IT?
Do we have Science in the afternoon?
How many subjects do we have in the morning?
How long is lunch?
Do we have Maths in the morning or the afternoon?
Is History the first lesson on Monday?
Is Religious Studies the last lesson?

Exercise D

Refer students back to the illustrations of the handouts.
1 Set for pairwork. Feed back, eliciting some ideas.
2 Explain that students are going to hear parts of five lessons. They must work out quickly which handout to look at in each case. Then they must complete the handout with information from the lesson. Set for individual work and pairwork checking.
Feed back, ideally onto an OHT of the completed handouts.

Tapescript

Presenter: **D 2 Listen and identify the lesson. Make notes on the correct handout.**

Voice: OK. Have you all got your Maths handout? Right. There's a drawing of a triangle. Do you know what kind of triangle it is? It's a right-angled triangle. That means one of the angles is ninety degrees. We show it with a square in the corner. Can you find the square? OK. That angle is ninety degrees. Write the number. Today, I'm going to explain how to find the area of a right-angled triangle. As you can see, this triangle has a base of six centimetres – can you all see the base? Six centimetres. And it has a height of ten centimetres. Now, how do you find the area? You multiply the base by the height. So that's six times ten, which is sixty square centimetres. And then you divide by two. So what's the area of this triangle? Write it on the handout.

This week in Geography we are going to look at Brazil. I've given you a map and I want you to label it. Brazil is a huge country, in area and in the number of people living there. There are two big cities on the east coast. The most famous city is Rio de Janeiro – that's in the south of the country, but north of Rio there is a much bigger city – São Paulo. Rio, that's R-I-O, has about twelve million people. But São Paulo, S-A-O P-A-U-L-O, has over twenty million. However, São Paulo is not the capital of Brazil. That's Brasilia, in the centre of the country. You spell it with an *s*, by the way, not a *z*. Brasilia is much smaller than Rio and São Paulo. The population in 2005 was three million, four hundred and fifty thousand. That's just under three and a half million …

So we've reached the 16th century in English History. There were two famous rulers in England in the 16th century. The first one was Henry VIII. You've got a picture of him there. We write *eighth* in a strange way with kings and queens. We use Roman numbers. So we write *five* with a capital *V*, then we need three capital *I*s. So *eighth* is VIII. Henry was king of England for thirty-eight years, from 1509 to 1547. Why is Henry so famous? Well, there are many reasons. But one reason is … he married six times. What happened to his six wives? Well, let's find out.

Right. In Science at the moment we are looking at colours. I've given you a drawing of a prism. It's like a pyramid made of glass. It's spelt P-R-I-S-M. As you can see, with a prism, white light comes in one side and all the colours of the rainbow come out the other side. Can you label all the colours?

OK. Last week we looked at flowcharts. Let's make sure we know the names of the different symbols. There's a simple flowchart on your handout. At the top is a rectangle with rounded corners. That's the Start box. So write *Start* in there. We use the same shape for the End box. So write *End* in that one. Now there are two other shapes here. Firstly, there are diamonds. The diamonds have two arrows coming out of them with *Yes* and *No* because you put questions in each diamond. So put a question mark in each one. Finally, there are three rectangles. These are Action boxes. So write *Action* in each rectangle – that's A-C-T-I-O-N.

Answers

Maths:
90°
30 cm²

Geography:
North – São Paulo
Centre – Brasilia
South – Rio de Janeiro

History:
(Henry) VIII

Science:
red, orange, yellow, green, indigo, violet

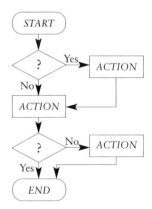

Closure

Walk round the class, saying words from the lesson and checking that individual students can point to the item. Make sure you do all the school subjects, but extend to include words from the 'lessons' such as *king, prism, triangle*, if you wish.

Lesson 2: Listening

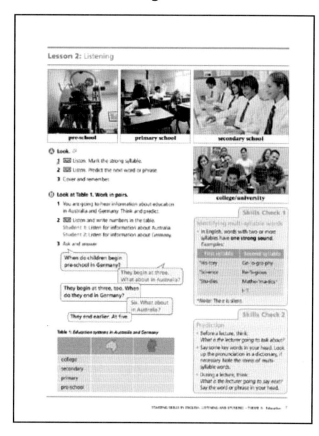

Science
1 How do you turn white light into all the colours of the rainbow? *put it through a prism*
2 What are the six colours – in order? *red, orange, yellow, green, indigo, violet*

IT
1 What does an Action box look like in a flowchart? *a rectangle*
2 What about a question box? *a diamond*

Geography
1 What is the capital of Brazil? *Brasilia*
2 How many people live in São Paulo? *20 million*

History
1 When did Henry VIII become king of England? *1509*
2 When did he die? *1547*

2 Say the names of the subjects, overstressing the stressed syllable and 'swallowing' the unstressed syllables. Get students to point to the correct subject handout again.

Introduction

1 See what students can remember from the 'lessons' in the last lesson. Put students into pairs or groups. Give them a quiz. Read out the questions – remember that this is a listening lesson! Tell them the subject area first in each case. Do not let them look at their books. They can discuss the answers and make some notes, but they must not give you the answers until the end of the quiz. Do not accept an answer unless it is well formed and well pronounced. Keep the score and declare a winning pair/group, if you wish.

Quiz
Maths
1 In a right-angled triangle, one angle is 90 degrees. True or false? *true*
2 How do you find out the area of a right-angled triangle? *half the base x the height*

Exercise A

Ask students to listen. Say the word *History*, emphasizing the stress on the first syllable. Write the word on the board, putting a small mark in front of the stressed syllable to indicate the stress. Repeat with *Science*, etc. Refer students to Skills Check 1.

1 Refer students to the pictures and words. Say or play the tape. Feed back, marking the stress correctly on each word.
2 Remind students, or tell them (see Methodology note 2 on page 19), that it is very important to stay ahead of a speaker by predicting what he/she is going to say next. This is part of active listening. Play the first sentence up to the pause to demonstrate the activity. Do not let students shout out the next word. Tell them to put up their hands if they think they know the next word. Hold the

pause until most students have put up their hands. Check ideas, then continue with the remainder.

3 Set for pairwork. Check comprehension by moving round and listening to pairs.

Methodology notes

1 Students may already be familiar with the concept of stress within words, and this method of marking it, from their previous learning.

2 There are many ways of marking stress within words – underlining, bolding, capitalizing, etc. However, dictionaries most often use the vertical stroke as in Skills Check 1, therefore it is good to teach students to understand and use this symbol for independent learning.

3 If students do not know about predicting content and the next word from their previous learning, refer them to the Skills Check at the end to fix these points.

Language and culture note

There are some complex rules for stress within words, but at this stage you can tell students to expect the stress on the first syllable of a two- or three-syllable noun. There are, of course, exceptions.

Tapescript

Presenter: Lesson 2
A 1 Listen. Mark the strong syllable.
Voice: 'pre-school
'primary
'secondary
'college
uni'versity

Presenter: A 2 Listen. Predict the next word or phrase.
Voice: Most countries in the world have four stages of education. The first stage is called [PAUSE] pre-school because *pre-* means *before*. At pre-school, children learn to play with other [PAUSE] children. In some countries, they start to learn how to read at [PAUSE] pre-school. The second stage is called [PAUSE] primary school because *primary* means [PAUSE] *first*. Primary school starts at [PAUSE] five or six in most countries. It ends at [PAUSE] ten, eleven or twelve. In some countries, children take a test at the end of [PAUSE] primary school. The next stage is called [PAUSE] secondary school. *Secondary* is the adjective from the word [PAUSE] *second*. Some children leave school at the end of [PAUSE] secondary. Other children go on to college or [PAUSE] university.

Exercise B

Refer students to the table. Ask a few checking questions. Put students into pairs.

1 Set for pairwork. Elicit a few ideas. Students should realize that they are going to hear numbers – ages – to be precise.

2 Set for individual work. Play the tape.

3 Set for pairwork. Work through the speech bubbles. Feed back, building up the complete table on the board.

Answers

	Australia	Germany
college	*18 or later*	*19/20*
secondary	*12/13–18*	*10–19*
primary	*5–12/13*	*6–10*
pre-school	*3–5*	*3–6*

Tapescript

Presenter: **B 2 Listen and write numbers in the table.**

Voice: Today, we are going to compare the education systems in two countries – Australia and Germany. There are four stages of education in both systems, and in both systems most children start pre-school at three. However, in Australia, pre-school ends at five years old, but in Germany it ends one year later, at six. Primary school in Australia begins at five and ends at twelve or thirteen, whereas in Germany, it goes from six to ten. Secondary school starts in Australia at twelve or thirteen, and finishes at eighteen. Most students then go on to university at eighteen, or perhaps later, after a break from studies. In Germany, secondary school lasts longer, from ten to nineteen. Then most students go on to university at nineteen or twenty.

Lesson 3: Speaking

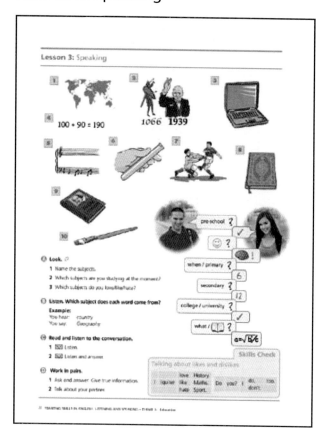

4 Say each pair of vowels for individual students to repeat.

5 Write the pair of words on the board, in a column marked *1* or *2* (see the tables).

6 Say the vowel sound of one of the two words from the pair. Students must say *1* or *2*.

7 As you do more and more pairs, go back over the previous pairs until you are saying sounds from random from the whole set.

Put students into pairs to do the minimal pairs activity below. Each student says one word from each pair and the other tries to work out which.

1	2
hard	had
turn	ten
leave	live
short	shot
pool	pull
no	now
wait	white

Introduction

Revise the main vowel sounds with words connected with education.

long vs short

1	2
ask	Maths
learn	lesson
speak	listen
taught	wrong
school	book

diphthongs

1	2
know	noun
say	write

Follow this procedure in each case.

1 Say each pair of words several times. Do not let students say anything.

2 Isolate the vowel sounds. Do not let students say anything.

3 Say each pair of vowels for students to repeat chorally.

Exercise A

1 Check that students can identify each of the subjects from the images. Drill the pronunciation, particularly the stressed syllable in the multi-syllable words.

2 Ask the question, individually, of as many students as possible. Obviously, if all the students are studying the same subjects, the return on this will be limited. Concentrate on the students who are struggling with the pronunciation of the subjects.

3 Refer them to the Skills Check and drill the sentences. Practise the exchanges with a good student. Put students into pairs to talk about the subjects.

Exercise B

Do this as a high-speed, whole-class activity, then repeat, nominating students to answer.

Teacher's script

Decide whether it is acceptable to use any of the words from Religious Studies.

Word	Subject
country	Geography
computer	IT
dates	History
football	Sport
God	Religious Studies
grammar	English
island	Geography
king	History
Koran	Religious Studies
Bible	Religious Studies
song	Music
programmer	IT
light	Science
map	Geography
numbers	Mathematics
painting	Art
tennis	Sport
vocabulary	English
printer	IT
sculpture	Art
singer	Music
south	Geography
swimming	Sport
triangle	Mathematics
vowel	English
table*	Science

*This refers to a data table.

Exercise C

Refer students to the pictures in the rebus conversation. Explain that these are reminders of sentences in the conversation. Students should look at the pictures while they are listening.
1   Play the tape.
2   Play the questions, pausing after each one for students to answer.

Tapescript

Presenter:	Lesson 3
	C 1 Listen.
Man:	Did you go to pre-school?
Woman:	Yes, I did.
Man:	Did you like it?
Woman:	I can't remember.
Man:	When did you start primary school?
Woman:	When I was six.
Man:	What about secondary school?
Woman:	I started when I was twelve.
Man:	Are you going to go to college or university?
Woman:	Yes, I think so.
Man:	What are you going to study?
Woman:	Maths, I think.

Presenter: **C 2 Listen and answer.**
Man: Did you go to pre-school?
[PAUSE]
Did you like it?
[PAUSE]
When did you start primary school?
[PAUSE]
What about secondary school?
[PAUSE]
Are you going to go to college or university?
[PAUSE]
What are you going to study?

Exercise D

Work through some of the alternative answers, as follows.
A: Did you go to pre-school?
B: *Yes, I did./No, I didn't.*

Clearly the next question can only be asked if the first answer is *Yes.*
A: Did you like it?
B: *I can't remember./Yes, I did.*
A: When did you start primary school?
B: *When I was five / six / seven.*
A: What about secondary school?
B: *I started when I was 10 / 11 / 12 / 13.*
A: Are you going to go to college or university?
B: *Yes, I think so./No, I don't think so.*

Clearly the next question can only be asked if the first answer is *Yes.*
A: What are you going to study?
B: *Maths/History,* etc., *I think.*

Drill the alternative answers. For the final answer, if necessary, help students to say what they are actually going to study.

Drill the questions. Make sure students recognize the two types: *Yes/No* and *Wh-*, but do not worry if the intonation is not perfect. There is more work on this later in the course.

1 Set for pairwork. Monitor and assist.
2 Ask students to tell you about their partner. Help with the extended turn.

Answer

Model answer:

Exercise D2
He went to pre-school at four, and primary school when he was six. He started secondary school at ten. He is going to go to university next year. He is going to study English.

Methodology notes

1 You are asking students to use a verb pattern here (*going to do*) which they have not formally studied in this course. If they have seen it in their previous learning, do not do a formal presentation. Just check that students are using /ə/ with *to*, i.e., *going ta study,* not *going to.*
2 Whenever you ask students to give true information about themselves, be prepared to spend some time with individuals, helping them find the correct word or words. This will enable them to build up a personal lexicon. For example, a student may be interested in studying psychology or anthropology or environmental science. If so, he or she needs the words now, not in three years' time when they have reached the correct level to learn that word or phrase in the natural course of language learning.

Closure

Reverse the activity from Exercise B. Say each subject and go round the class eliciting as many words connected with that subject as possible. Correct vowel sounds particularly as you go.

Lesson 4: Speaking

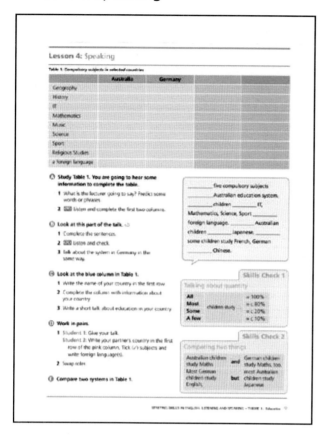

Introduction

Write *The Alphabet Game* on the board. Elicit the alphabet, in the correct order and with good pronunciation of each letter. Ask students to try to think of a word connected with education, beginning with each letter of the alphabet. They should at least know and be able to say the following words.

Answers
Possible answers:

A *adjective, answer, ask*
B *book*
C *chair, class, college*
D *desk*
E *education, exercise*
F *find*
G *Geography, grammar*
H *History, homework*
I *IT*
J *?*
K *?*
L *lesson, listen*
M *Maths*
N *notebook, notes, noun*
O *?*
P *primary, pronoun*
Q *question*
R *read, right*
S *say, school, Science, secondary, spell*
T *test*
U *university*
V *verb*
W *write, wrong*
X *?*
Y *?*
Z *?*

Exercise A

Refer students to the table. Explain *compulsory*, i.e., all children do this. It is the law. Ask students about the compulsory subjects in their school system(s). Ask them which foreign languages Australian and German students might learn.

1 Set for pairwork. Feed back. Students should be able to predict sentences like *In Australia, children study … They don't study …*

2 Set for individual work and pairwork checking. Play the tape. Feed back, ideally onto an OHT of the table.

Answers

	Australia	Germany
Geography		
History		✓
IT	✓	
Mathematics	✓	✓
Music		
Science	✓	✓
Sport	✓	✓
Religious Studies		
a foreign language	✓ *Japanese, French, German or Chinese*	✓ *English*

Tapescript

Presenter: Lesson 4

A 2 Listen and complete the first two columns.

Voice: There are five compulsory subjects in the Australian education system. All children study IT, Mathematics, Science, Sport and a foreign language. Most Australian children study Japanese, but some children study French, German or Chinese. There are five compulsory subjects in the German education system, too. Four subjects are the same. All students study Mathematics, Science, Sport and a foreign language. Most German children study English. One subject is different. German children study History, not IT.

Methodology notes

1 Students should remember the spelling of the language/nationality words, or at least make an attempt to spell them.
2 There is very little redundancy in this short text. This is deliberate. When people are listing, as here, listeners have to process the items in the list very quickly.

Language and culture note

Students may not be aware that most Australians speak English as a first language and, therefore, may think that English will be the foreign language. They may also not realize where Australia is – its geographic position explains the importance of Japanese and Chinese as foreign languages.

Exercise B

This exercise focuses on the function rather than the content words. Refer students to Skills Check 1. Check comprehension and drill the expressions. Get students to make some true sentences about children in their own education system(s).

By this point, they should have forgotten the carrier words and phrases and, therefore, have to work them out from the context.
1 Set for individual work and pairwork checking.
2 Play the first part of the talk again.
3 Set for pairwork, monitor and assist.

Tapescript

Presenter: **B 2 Listen and check.**

Voice: There are five compulsory subjects in the Australian education system. All children study IT, Mathematics, Science, Sport and a foreign language. Most Australian children study Japanese, but some children study French, German or Chinese.

Exercise C

Set for individual work. Monitor and assist.

Exercise D

Set for pairwork. Monitor and assist.

Exercise E

Set for pairwork.

If students are from the same country, ask them to compare their system with either Australia or Germany. Otherwise, ask students to compare the two systems they come from.

Refer students to Skills Check 2. Work through these basic ways of comparing with *and* and *but*. Point out the use of *too*.

Methodology note

Inevitably, comparison sentences are quite long. Help students to get through the sentence by pointing out that you can pause after the linking word, *and/but*, to gather your thoughts for the second half.

Closure

Make sure students can say all the target words from this theme with good pronunciation, particularly word stress and pronunciation of vowels.

THEME 2 Daily Life

General note

By the end of this theme, students should be able to hear and identify, in isolation and in context, the following words linked with daily life. They should also be able to say them with reasonable pronunciation, especially stress in multi-syllable words, and use them in simple S V (O) (C) sentences with frequency adverbs and phrases.

always	midnight	past	tomorrow
autumn	minute	quarter (time)	tonight
early	never	season	winter
half	noon	sometimes	yesterday
late	o'clock	spring	
later	often	summer	

They should also be able to talk about regular events with the following verbs:

wake up
get up
have breakfast/lunch
leave home
get to school/college
leave school/college
get home
watch television, etc.
go to bed

Lesson 1: Listening

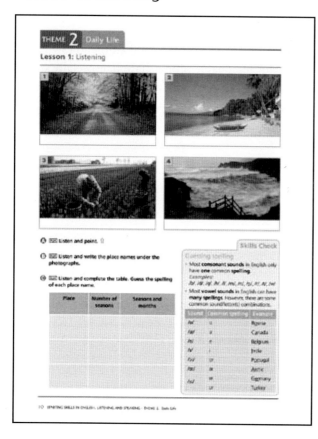

1 Get students to tell you the times of each part of the day.
2 Get them to tell you the hour, the day today, and the current month.
3 Give a day or month at random and get students to tell you the next one and the last one.

When you have gone through the words once, repeat at high speed.

Then put some, or all, of the words into sentence context.

Exercise A

Refer students to the pictures. Ask them what they can see. Elicit any vocabulary items they know, but do not insist on other students saying or understanding the words. They should all be able to name some of the items and most of the colours. Explain that they are going to hear about times of the year in Europe, North America, China and Japan. Point to the map and say *Europe is in the Northern Hemisphere*. Then mime what this means. Check the concept by asking *Where is Australia?* (in the Southern Hemisphere), and other countries at random. Point to them on the map.

Tell students to point to the correct picture. Say or play the first word – *summer* – as an example. Make sure all the students are pointing to picture 2. Say or play the tape. Watch the class and try to identify any student who is not correctly associating the spoken word with the picture.

You can go through this activity several times, speeding up and saying words and individual sentences in a different order.

At the end, teach the word *season* as the hyponym.

Introduction

Take in a large map of the world so, at the appropriate time, you can point to parts of the world, e.g., the Northern Hemisphere, continents, e.g., Europe, and individual countries. Stick the map to the wall, board or noticeboard, so it is permanently displayed.

Students may already be familiar with the following words from this lexical set:

afternoon	hour	night	week
day	last	now	year
evening	month	time	
first	morning	today	

They should also be fluent in the days of the week and the months of the year. If you are in any doubt, check that all the students can identify and produce these words in isolation.

Tapescript

Presenter: Theme 2 Daily Life
Lesson 1
A Listen and point.

Voice: summer
winter
spring
autumn

Voices: The trees are turning brown. It's not cold, but it's not hot. It's autumn.

It is very hot. The sun is shining and the sky is always blue. It's summer.

It's very cold and wet. There are often storms. The sea is sometimes very rough. It's winter.

The fields are full of flowers. It is not hot, but it is not cold. It's spring.

In the Northern Hemisphere, summer is June, July and August.

Autumn is September, October and November.

Winter is December to February.

Spring starts in March and ends in May.

Methodology note

It is likely that students will not know all the season words, but they will almost certainly know *summer* and *winter*. By starting with these, we give them the chance to work out the others.

Language and culture note

This is a listening lesson, so the point may not arise, but we do not normally capitalize seasons, unless we are personalizing them as in *Where are the songs of Spring? Ay, where are they?*

Remember not to use a capital letter if you write any of these words on the board.

Exercise B

Ask students to guess which country is shown in each picture. Elicit some ideas, but do not confirm or correct. Explain that they are going to hear the names of the places and they will have to guess the spelling. Point out that speakers often name places and you have to work out the spelling. Explain that you can guess the spelling if you follow some simple patterns.

Refer students to the Skills Check. Work through the consonant sounds which lead to one consonant letter in most cases. Elicit the letter, which is the same as the shape inside the obliques.

Then work through the sound/common spellings of some vowel sounds.

Say or play the sentences.

Answers
1   Vermont, USA
2   Barbados, West Indies
3   Amsterdam, Holland
4   Cornwall, Britain

Tapescript

Presenter: B Listen and write the place names under the photographs.

Voice: The photograph of winter shows a storm in Cornwall, in Britain.

The summer photograph was taken in Barbados, in the West Indies.

Do you like this picture of spring? I took it in Amsterdam, in Holland.

There is a song called *Autumn in Vermont*. They say it's the most beautiful place in the world at that time of year. This photograph shows the lovely autumn colours in Vermont, in the USA.

Methodology note

Point out that you cannot necessarily guess the full spelling of proper nouns – towns, cities, countries, people – because one sound can have different spellings, e.g.,

Bos/Boz nia

C/K anada

Bel g/jium

Denmar c/k

G/J ermany

Tur c/k ey

However, that is fine because, by following the patterns, you can narrow down the spelling, then check in an atlas or encyclopedia.

Language and culture note

The following consonant sounds are missing from the list of consonants because of two or more common spellings:

/f/ = f or p, and even v, in *have to*

/ʤ/ = g or j

/k/ = k or c

/s/ = c or s

/v/ = f or v

/z/ = s or z (as in *is, has, was, his*)

Exercise C

Refer students to the table. Explain that they are going to hear information to complete it. Ask them to guess some of the words they are going to hear. Clearly, they should realize that numbers, months and seasons will be mentioned, but elicit also *cold, hot, wet*. Check or teach *cool* as between *cold* and *hot*.

Say or play the first part of the tape and show the way that students can try to guess the spelling of *Islamabad*, i.e., *Izlamabad*, then point out that it is *Islamabad*. Set for individual work and pairwork checking.

Play the remainder of the tape. Feed back, building up the table on the board. Show how single letters can be used to note months, except *M* and *J*. Be prepared to show students where the countries are on the map. Go through alternative spellings based on sound, e.g., *Nigeria* could be *Nij* …

Answers

Place	Number of seasons	Seasons and months
Islamabad, Pakistan	*4*	*cold = D–Mar* *hot = A–June* *wet = July–S* *cool = O–N*
Baga, Nigeria	*2*	*dry = O–A* *wet = M–S*
Nazca, Peru	*2*	*summer = D–Mar* *winter = A–N*

Tapescript

Presenter: C Listen and complete the table. Guess the spelling of each place name.

Voice: Most parts of the world have four seasons. For example, Islamabad, which is the capital of Pakistan, has a cold season, a hot season, a wet season and a cool season. The cold season is from December to the end of March. The hot season is from the beginning of April to June. The wet season is from July to September. Finally, the cool season starts in October and ends in November. Some parts of the world only have two seasons. For example, Baga, which is in the north of Nigeria, in Africa, has a dry season and a wet season. The dry season is from October to April. The wet season is from May to September. Baga is in the Northern Hemisphere. But some places in the Southern Hemisphere also have two seasons. For example, Nazca in Peru, which is in South America, has a summer season and a winter season. The summer season is from December to March, and the winter season from April to November.

Closure

Walk round the class, saying words from the lesson and checking that individual students can point to the item. Ask also about the months depicted in particular pictures. Remind students that all these places are in the Northern Hemisphere.

Lesson 2: Listening

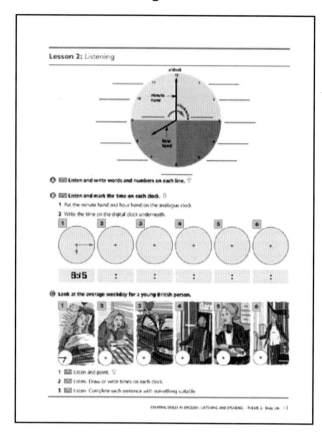

Introduction

Ideally, take in one or more teaching clocks so that you can say times and get students to move the hands accordingly.

Take in the world map again. Point out countries. Dictate the names for students to try to guess. Possible countries:

Benin	Finland	Niger
Chad	Gambia	Yemen
Chile	Honduras	Oman
Dominica	Iran (/iræn/)	Iraq

Language and culture note

The way a language chooses to write the name of another country is largely historical and may not accord with the way the language of that culture refers to itself. Students need to learn the spelling of most, or arguably all, countries in the world in English, and the first stage is guessing from the common sound-sight spelling patterns.

Exercise A

Ask students to identify the drawing. Check or teach *clock*. Get students to name the numbers around the clock. Make sure they go clockwise, i.e., *1, 2, 3*, etc. Point out that this is *clockwise*. Get students to show clockwise and anti-/counter-clockwise movement with their hands. Get students to point to the minute hand. Ask *How many minutes in an hour?* Get students to point to the hour hand. Ask *How many hours in a day?*

Set for individual work and pairwork checking. Say or play the tape.

Answers

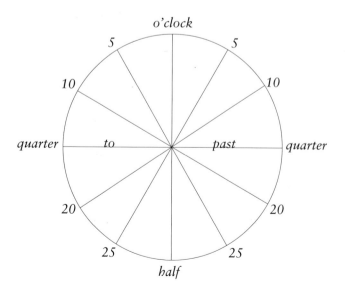

Tapescript

Presenter: Lesson 2
A Listen and write words and numbers on each line.

Voice: This is a clock. There is a minute hand and an hour hand. The hour hand points to the hour, and the minute hand points to the minutes. When the minute hand points to twelve, we say o'clock. For example, this clock shows eight o'clock. Times on the right side of the clock are *past*, that's P-A-S-T, and times on the left side are *to*. That's T-O, not T-W-O. When the minute hand points to one, it's five past, and when it points to two, it's ten past. There is a special word for three. It's *quarter*. That's Q-U-A-R-T-E-R. Four is twenty past, and five is twenty-five past. There is another special word for six. We say *half past*. The numbers and words on the left side are the same as the numbers on the right side. So we have twenty-five to, twenty to, quarter to, ten to and five to. OK. So now you can tell the time in English.

Language and culture notes

1 Many teenagers of all cultures can no longer tell analogue time, even in their own language. They work constantly with digital time and, therefore, get used to saying, e.g., in English *It's ten ten*, rather than *It's ten past ten*. Many do not even round up or down, so say, e.g., *It's nine thirteen*. Bear in mind, therefore, that in teaching telling the time in this way, you may be teaching a concept rather than a language point.
2 The suffix *-wise* means 'in the manner (or way) of'.
3 Speakers of British English tend to say *anti-clockwise*, while speakers of American English tend to say *counter-clockwise*.

Exercise B

Refer students to the first clock face. Say or play the tape and show students how they can mark the time by drawing the long minute hand and the shorter hour hand.
1 Set for individual work and pairwork checking. Feed back, ideally with a teaching clock. Get students to say the times they have drawn using *past, to, quarter* and *half*.
2 Now get students to complete the digital times.

Methodology note

If it is clear that all or many of your students are struggling with the idea of drawing hands on clocks, allow them to complete the digital times instead. The comprehension point has still been served – understanding time said in this analogue way.

Answers

1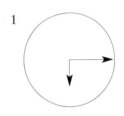

4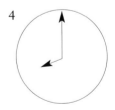

2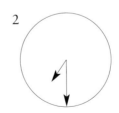

5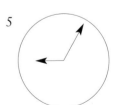

3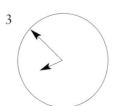

6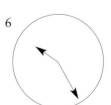

Tapescript

Presenter: **B Listen and mark the time on each clock.**

Voice: 1 quarter past six
2 half past seven
3 ten to eight
4 eight o'clock
5 five past nine
6 twenty-five past ten

Exercise C

Refer students to the pictures. Explain that this is what the average British person does every weekday. This information comes from a survey of the daily life of people in ten European countries. Make sure students understand *weekday* as opposed to *weekend*. Elicit actions in the pictures, but do not confirm or correct.

1 Say or play the first action. Check that students are pointing to the right picture by asking, after a long pause, for the number. Keep control of strong/voluble students shouting out before others have had a chance to think. Say or play the remaining items. Add mimes to the words during a second playing.

2 Say or play the first part of the tape. Get students to recognize the relationship between the first action and the time. Say or play the remainder of the text, pausing if necessary for students to complete the times. Feed back, by reading the tapescript and pausing at the relevant times, e.g., *The average young British person wakes up at ... quarter to seven.*

3 Remind students of the importance of predicting the next word or phrase. Say or play the tape, pausing where marked for students to suggest possible words or phrases. As before, allow time for students to think before inviting answers.

Methodology note

If you can use simple mime without getting embarrassed, you will greatly benefit a large proportion of your students who need to associate learning with something physical.

Language and culture note

If you are a native speaker of English, or from a Western European country, it is tempting to teach the weekend by adding *you know, Saturday and Sunday*. However, this will just be confusing for students who come from a culture with a different weekend. The weekend is a day or days you do not work, not a specific day or days of the week.

Tapescript

Presenter: **C 1 Listen and point.**

Voice: She has breakfast.
She arrives at work.
She finishes work.
She has lunch, then she goes shopping.
She leaves home.
She wakes up.

Presenter: **C 2 Listen. Draw or write times on each clock.**

Voice: The average young British person wakes up at quarter to seven. She gets up at seven o'clock. She has breakfast at quarter past seven. She eats cereal and drinks coffee. She leaves home at twenty past eight and drives to work. It takes twenty minutes. She gets to work at twenty to nine and starts work at nine. She has a break from quarter to one to quarter to two, but she often stays at her desk. She has a sandwich and a cup of coffee. She sometimes goes shopping. She never goes to a restaurant. She finishes work at five o'clock and drives home.

Presenter: **C 3 Listen. Complete each sentence with something suitable.**

Voice: In the evening, she sometimes watches television and she sometimes goes to [PAUSE] a sports centre. She often cooks a meal, but sometimes she [PAUSE] gets a takeaway pizza. Once a week, she visits [PAUSE] her parents. She goes to bed at [PAUSE] quarter past ten.

On Saturday, she always goes [PAUSE] shopping. On Saturday evening, she [PAUSE] meets friends. She goes to bed later, at [PAUSE] eleven thirty. On Sunday, she always gets up [PAUSE] late, at nine or nine thirty. She does [PAUSE] housework. In the evening, she [PAUSE] watches television and [PAUSE] gets ready for work.

She never sleeps [PAUSE] in the afternoon, even at weekends.

Closure

Refer students back to the pictures in Lesson 1. Ask students about the seasons in their country: *What time does the sun rise and set in winter, spring, summer and autumn?* If necessary, mime or draw sunrise and sunset. If there is a big difference in sunset times, ask if they do different things in the evening in summer and in winter.

Lesson 3: Speaking

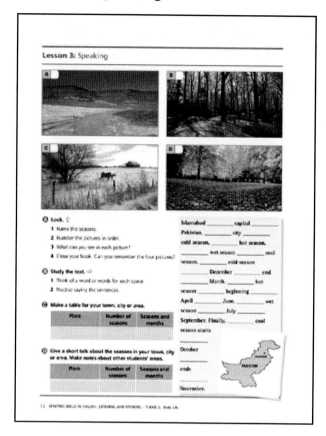

Introduction

Use the world map from Lesson 1. Revise the main vowel sounds with country names.

long vs short	
1	2
France	Chad
Germany	Denmark
Greece	Libya
Portugal	Holland
Peru	Cook (Islands)

diphthongs	
1	2
Angola	Laos
Ukraine	China

Follow this procedure in each case.

1 Say each pair of words several times. Do not let students say anything.
2 Isolate the vowel sounds. Do not let students say anything.

3 Say each pair of vowels for students to repeat chorally.
4 Say each pair of vowels for individual students to repeat.
5 Write the pair of words on the board, in a column marked *1* or *2* (see the tables).
6 Say the vowel sound of one of the two words from the pair. Students must say *1* or *2*.
7 As you do more and more pairs, go back over the previous pairs until you are saying sounds from random from the whole set.

Put students into pairs to do the minimal pairs activity below. Each student says one word from each pair and the other tries to work out which. Point out that these are all English words, although the meanings are not important.

1	2
part	pat
pert	pet
Pete	pit
port	pot
pool	pull
po	pow!
paint	pint

Exercise A

1 Check that students can identify each of the subjects from the images. Drill the pronunciation, particularly the unusual sound-sight relationship of /ɔː/ (*au* in *autumn*).
2 Elicit the 'correct' order.
3 Work through the spring picture as an example, using *I can see/There is* and *The X is Y* structures. Set for pairwork. Monitor and assist. Feed back, eliciting as much as possible with reasonable structure and pronunciation, about each picture.
4 Set for pairwork. One student is allowed to look at the book while the other tries to remember. Practise expressions for location on a page – *top left, bottom right*, etc.

Methodology note

Take the opportunity to practise the present continuous.

Exercise B

Refer students to the map of Pakistan. Show where Pakistan is on the world map. Elicit some ideas or knowledge on seasons.
1 Work through the first few spaces as examples. Set for individual work and pairwork checking. Do not let students write anything. You may need to teach *cool*.
2 Allow students to read sentences aloud, putting in the missing words. Drill for form and pronunciation. Remind students about structural points as you go, e.g., countries do not need the definite article. Remind students also of semantic points, e.g., we use *the* for the second time: *a cold season – the cold season.*

Answers

Islamabad *is the* capital *of* Pakistan. *The* city *has a* cold season, *a* hot season, *a* wet season *and a* cool season. *The* cold season *is from* December *to the* end *of* March. *The* hot season *is from the* beginning *of* April *to* June. *The* wet season *is from* July *to* September. Finally, *the* cool season starts *in* October *and* ends *in* November.

Methodology note

Note that students do not have to write in this exercise. This means that they have to remember the structure rather than simply copy it when they come to Exercise D.

Exercise C

Build up on the board a model table for Pakistan from the information in the text.

Set for individual work and pairwork checking. Point out that students will have to guess/work out the number of seasons and start/finish months. They can refer to them as *hot, cold*, etc., or as *summer, winter*, etc.

Answers

Model notes for Pakistan:

Place	Number of seasons	Seasons and months
Islamabad, Pakistan	*4*	*cold – D–Mar* *hot – A–June* *wet – July–S* *cool – O–N*

Language and culture note

Allow students to use month names from their own culture, if they wish. Arab students will have to use English names, however, as the months are lunar and their position changes by about ten days each year.

Exercise D

Students can work in pairs or small groups if they come from the same town, city or area.

Put students into small groups to give their talks. The listeners must make notes in their notebooks. Monitor and assist.

Closure

Get students to ask you about your own town, city or area to elicit the information required to complete the tables in this lesson, e.g.,
> *Where do you live?*
> *Where is that?/Which country is that in?*
> *How many seasons do you have?*
> *What are they called?*
> *When does (season 1) start/finish?*

Lesson 4: Speaking

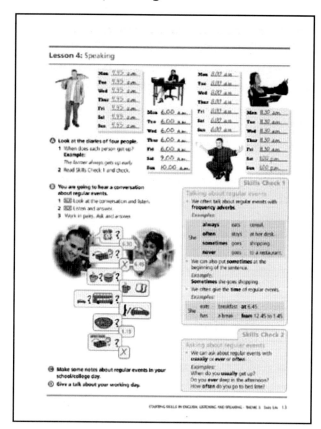

Introduction

Ask students in turn to tell you the:

    year

    season

    month

    day

    time

Ask students to tell you the same information for:

    last year

    last month

    yesterday

Repeat for:

    next year

    next month

    tomorrow

Tell students about yourself and getting up, e.g., *I get up at 6.30 every day.* Ask students when they get up.

Elicit some times until it is clear that everyone understands the idea.

Exercise A

Refer students to the diary pages. Exploit the visuals. Find a way to refer to each person, e.g., the farmer, the commuter, the paper boy, the actress.

1 Give all the students time to think about the answer, then elicit. Write the frame sentence on the board: *He/She ... gets up early.* Elicit possible completions. Do not confirm or correct, but edge them towards the target – the list of frequency adverbs and the semantic value of each adverb. If students are struggling with this, write the first letter of each word in the set, in order, on the board. Also say *one hundred percent, seventy percent,* etc.

2 Refer students to Skills Check 1. Get students to try again to make a full sentence with a frequency adverb about each of the people. Drill the pronunciation of the frequency adverbs.

Answers

The farmer – he always gets up early.

The commuter – she often gets up early.

The paperboy – he sometimes gets up early.

The actress – she never gets up early.

Exercise B

Refer students to the pictures. Explain that these are reminders of sentences in the conversation. They should look at the pictures while they are listening.

1 Play the tape.

2 Play the questions, pausing after each one for the students to answer. Refer students to Skills Check 2. Drill the questions, noting the intonation patterns.

3 Put students in pairs to role play the conversation, giving information from the pictures, not true information for them.

Tapescript

Presenter: Lesson 4

B 1 **Look at the conversation and listen.**

Man: When do you usually wake up?

Woman: At half past six.

Man: Do you get up immediately?

Woman: No. I get up at about quarter to seven.

Man: What do you usually have for breakfast?

Woman: I always have coffee and two pieces of toast.

Man: How do you get to school?

Woman: Sometimes I walk and sometimes I go by car.

Man: What time do you have lunch?

Woman: At quarter past one.

Man: Do you ever sleep in the afternoon?

Woman: No, I don't. I never sleep in the afternoon.

Presenter: B 2 **Listen and answer.**

Man: When do you usually wake up?
[PAUSE]
Do you get up immediately?
[PAUSE]
What do you usually have for breakfast?
[PAUSE]
How do you get to school?
[PAUSE]
What time do you have lunch?
[PAUSE]
Do you ever sleep in the afternoon?

Language and culture note

We can answer a question about frequency in two main ways, e.g.,

Do you ever sleep in the afternoon?
No, never./Yes, always., etc.

OR

No, I don't.

Students tend to mix this up and produce *No, I never.*

Exercise C

Set for individual work. Make sure students realize that on this occasion they are thinking about school/college days, not weekends. Monitor and assist.

Exercise D

Put students into pairs or small groups to give their talk. Feed back by getting one or two of the best ones to give their talk to the whole class.

Closure

Make sure students can say all the target words from this theme with good pronunciation, particularly word stress and pronunciation of vowels.

THEME 3 Work and Business

General note

By the end of this theme, students should be able to hear and identify, in isolation and in context, the following words linked with work and business. They should also be able to say them with reasonable pronunciation, especially stress in multi-syllable words, and use them in simple S V (O) (C) sentences.

agriculture	file	manual	transport
company	finance	manufacturing	worker
construction	government	professional	working hours
employ	leisure	retail	
employment	manager	supermarket	

Lesson 1: Listening

Introduction

Students may already be familiar with the following words from this lexical set:

accountant	lawyer
bank	office
computer	receptionist
court	secretary
doctor	shop
engineer	start
factory	typist
hospital	want
hotel	work (n)
job	work (v)

If you are in any doubt, check that all the students can identify and produce these words in isolation.

1   Say relevant words from the list above and get students to say *job* or *place* or *verb*.

2   When you have gone through the words once, repeat at high speed.

Then put some, or all, of the words into sentence context.

Exercise A

Refer students to the pictures. Ask them what they can see. Elicit any vocabulary items they know, but do not insist on other students saying or understanding the words. They should all be able to name some of the items and most of the colours.

Explain that they are going to hear words connected with jobs. Tell students to point to the correct picture. Say or play the first word – *bank* – as an example. Make sure all the students are pointing to picture A. Say or play the tape of the individual words. Watch the students and try to identify any student who is not correctly associating the spoken word with the picture.

You can go through this activity several times, speeding up and saying words and individual sentences in a different order.

Tapescript

Presenter:		**Theme 3 Work and Business**
		Lesson 1
		A Listen and point.
Voices:	1	bank
	2	computer
	3	factory
	4	hotel
	5	houses
	6	office
	7	receptionist
	8	architect
	9	ship
	10	shop
	11	train
	12	trees
	13	typist

Refer students to Skills Check 1 – on the facing page. Check that they understand the concept. Then say or play the first two sentences as examples. Say or play the rest.

Tapescript

Presenter:		Skills Check 1
		Listen.
Voices:	1	Are you intending to be a doctor?
	2	Does your work involve using a computer?
	3	Are you going to the shops at lunchtime?
	4	He works in a factory.
	5	I don't want to work in an office.
	6	I love old houses.
	7	I'm going to go by train.
	8	International Hotel are looking for receptionists.
	9	After school, I worked as a typist for a few months.
	10	It's a nice hotel.
	11	She works in a bank.
	12	The trees are beautiful in autumn.
	13	When does the ship sail?

Methodology note

Good language learners are risk-takers. They put themselves into situations where they cannot possibly understand everything which is said, but they learn to cope with the situation. Poor language learners need to be shown that they can understand what is being said, without knowing every word. This activity begins to build the necessary skill of not panicking when they hear language they do not understand.

Exercise B

Say the word *employ*. Say that it means 'give someone a job'. So *employer* means 'someone who gives you a job'. *Employment* means 'jobs'. Remind students that there are many different kinds of jobs. We can see different kinds in the pictures. Now we are going to hear the names for the different kinds of jobs – the different *employment sectors*.

Refer students to Skills Check 2. Say or play the first two sentences. They are the ones in the Examples in the Skills Check. Work through the examples. Point out that *Finance* and the *Leisure industry* are two employment sectors.

Ask students to point at the correct picture as soon as they understand. This might be at the beginning of each extract, the middle, or the end.

Say or play the remaining items. Watch to see how quickly students are pointing.

Tapescript

Presenter:	B	Listen. What is the name for each employment sector?
Voices:	1	A lot of people work in Finance, for example, Banking.
	2	They work in the Leisure industry. She is a hotel receptionist and he is a sports teacher.
	3	There are fewer jobs in Manufacturing nowadays. Many factories are closing.
	4	The Transport industry is very important in every country. Factories make things, but ships, trains, planes and lorries are needed to move them to the shops.
	5	I am in the Retail trade. Well, actually, I work in a shop.

6 Very few people work in Agriculture in the UK nowadays. People are leaving the country and moving to towns.

7 He works for a big construction company. They build houses. He is an architect.

8 I work as a clerk in a Government office. My office pays money to people who haven't got a job.

Exercise C

Explain that students are only going to hear the sector names now. They must try to point to the correct picture in each case. Play the first two as examples, then the remaining items. Allow students to help each other to point to the correct picture.

Tapescript

Presenter:	**C Listen and point to the employment sector.**
Voice:	Agriculture
	Construction
	Finance
	Government
	the Leisure industry
	Manufacturing
	the Retail trade
	the Transport industry

Methodology note

Students might struggle with this, so have an OHT or the page ready for datashow. Then you can say or play the tape and point at the correct picture yourself, then try to get students to do it by themselves again.

Exercise D

Refer students to Table 1 and check that they understand that the icons represent the different employment sectors. Ask some quick checking questions about the information in the table, e.g.,

What country is this about? (The UK)
Is this information true now? (Probably. Note that this was Winter 2003.)
Who collected the information? (Labour Market Trends)
When did they print the information? (June 2004)
How many different sectors are shown? (Seven, or eight if you count 'other'.)
Why is the total 100? (Because this is percentages.)

Set for individual work and pairwork checking. Say or play the first sentence of the lecture. Make sure students have identified the correct sector and have written a number.

Feed back by saying a sector and getting a number. Do not ask students to say the sector names at this stage.

Point out that the final table is difficult to read in this form. It would be much easier to arrange it with the largest percentage (*Government*) at the top and the lowest at the bottom. However, it is probably better to put *other* at the very bottom, so *Agriculture* comes just above.

Answers

Sector	%
Agriculture	1
Manufacturing	15
Construction	6
Leisure and Retail	20
Transport	7
Finance	16
Government	28
other	7
Total	100

Tapescript

Presenter: **D Listen and complete Table 1.**

Lecturer: Do most people in your country work in Manufacturing? Or do they work in Agriculture? What about Construction? According to a survey by Labour Market Trends in June 2004, most people in the UK work for the Government. Does that seem strange? Remember, most doctors and nurses work for the Government. Most teachers in schools, colleges and universities work for the Government. And of course, there are many clerks and typists in local Government offices. Twenty-eight percent of people in the UK work for the Government in one way or another.

In second place, we have the Leisure and Retail industries. Britain is a popular holiday destination, and twenty percent of people work in hotels, restaurants and shops.

Finance is in third place. Sixteen percent of people work in banks, insurance companies, etc., closely followed by Manufacturing.

At one time, most people in Britain worked on a farm, in a factory or down a coal mine, but now only fifteen percent of jobs are in Manufacturing, and only one percent are in Agriculture. After Manufacturing, we have Transport at seven percent, and Construction at six percent. Other industries, like Fishing, make up the remaining seven percent.

Closure

Ask the question from the beginning of the lecture and see if students can answer with *Yes* or *No*, i.e.,

You say: *Do most people work in Agriculture?*

Students say: *Yes./No.*

You say: *Do they work in Manufacturing?*, etc.

Lesson 2: Listening

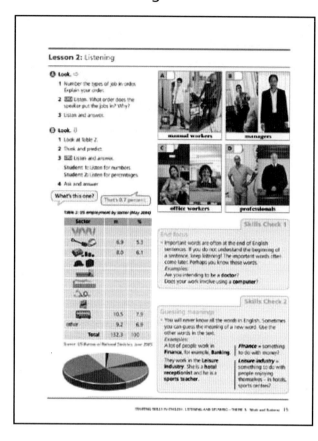

Introduction

Take in magazine pictures which are representative of different employment sectors as follows: Agriculture, Manufacturing, Construction, Leisure, Retail, Transport, Finance, Government.

If you have magazine pictures, hold up each picture and say an employment sector. If it matches the picture, students say *Yes*. Otherwise, they say *No*. If you do not have magazine pictures, do the same with the pictures from Lesson 1.

Exercise A

Refer students to the pictures, but do not let them try to say the names of the types of job.
1. Say *There are four main types of job. Put the types of jobs in order.* Do not explain how to do this. Set for pairwork. Feed back, accepting any reasonable order, for example, students might do it on the basis of money, interest, danger, needing English!

2. Say or play the tape. Feed back, eliciting the speaker's order and reason.
3. Ask some checking questions on the information students heard and can see in the pictures, e.g.,
   What are the four main types of jobs?
   Which type often gets the best salary?
   Can you name some manual jobs?, etc.
   Do not let students shout out answers.

Answers
1. Depend on the students.
2. The speaker puts them in this order:
   A4, B1, C3, D2. He points out, however, that professionals can get more than managers, and manual workers can be the highest paid.
3. Depend on the students.

Tapescript

Presenter: Lesson 2
A 2 Listen. What order does the speaker put the jobs in? Why?

Lecturer: There are four main kinds of job. In many employment sectors, managers get better salaries than other employees. They often have more interesting jobs than other people, too. However, in some countries, professionals, like doctors and lawyers, earn a lot of money. Office workers, such as typists, secretaries and clerks, come next in order of pay with manual workers, for example, construction workers or cleaners, at the bottom. However, in some countries, manual workers, like miners, get better salaries than office workers or even managers.

Exercise B

Refer students to Table 2. Ask checking questions.
1, 2 Remind students about the importance of predicting before you listen. They should have some idea of what the percentage, and therefore

total numbers, might be. Elicit some ideas, but do not confirm or correct.

3 Put students in pairs. Make sure students realize what they have to do. Play the tape up to the first number and percentage.

4 Explain how students can give each other the missing information. Work through the language they can use without having to say the actual sectors.

Monitor and assist. Feed back, building up the table on the board.

Answers

Sector	m	%
Agriculture	1.0	0.7
Construction	6.9	5.3
Finance	8.0	6.1
Government	21.6	16.3
Leisure	12.5	9.4
Manufacturing	14.3	10.8
Professionals	33.3	25.2
Retail	15.0	11.4
Transport	10.5	7.9
other	9.2	6.9
Total	132.3	100

Tapescript

Presenter: B 3 Listen and answer.

Lecturer: Which sector of the US economy is the biggest employer? At one time, it was Agriculture. At another time it was Manufacturing. Many people think it is the Government now. But in fact, Professionals are the biggest employment sector. According to figures from the US Bureau of National Statistics, in May 2004, there were thirty-three point three million professionals out of a total employment of one hundred and thirty-two point three million. That's twenty-five point two percent. The Government is a big employer. It employs sixteen point three percent of all workers, a total of twenty-one point six million

people. In third place, we have the Retail trade which is bigger than Manufacturing now. The Retail trade employs fifteen million people, or eleven point four percent. Manufacturing is slightly smaller. There are fourteen point three million people in Manufacturing, or ten point eight percent. The Leisure industry is next with twelve point five million, or nine point four percent. Then we have Transport, Finance, and Construction, in that order. So in last place, we have Agriculture, with just one million people – that's nought point seven percent of total employment.

Methodology note

The use of deictics in this way is one of the targets of this theme. Make sure the semantic point is clear, i.e., *this* = near me, *that* = away from me/near you.

Closure

Set the pie chart as a puzzle. Students have to work out which sector is which colour, and write the first letter of the sector on the pie chart. Once again, they can use deictic reference, rather than the actual word, e.g., *I think this one … is this one.* Feed back, saying the employment sectors and colours. Point out that some are very similar, so it is not really possible to be sure.

Answers

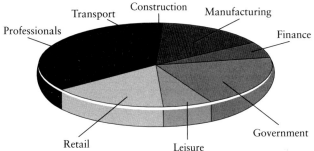

Lesson 3: Speaking

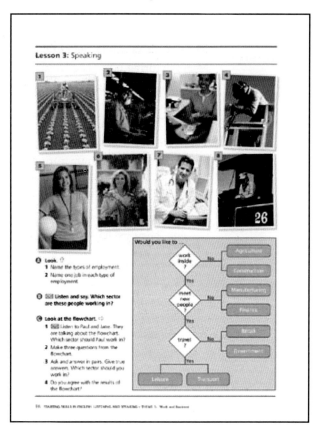

Introduction

Revise the main vowel sounds with words connected with work and business.

long vs short
(based on the stressed syllable in each case)

1	2		1	2
clerk	bank		court	job
farm	transport			shop
	manufacturing			doctor
	factory			office
	agriculture			hospital
	manual		computer	construction
	manager		use	government
work	leisure			money
worker	professional			
nurse	secretary			
retail	ship			
engineer				
teacher				

diphthongs

1	2
hotel	accountant
train	finance
	typist

Follow this procedure in each case.

1 Say a word from each pair several times, e.g., *clerk – bank*. Do not let students say anything.
2 Isolate the vowel sounds. Do not let students say anything.
3 Say each pair of stressed vowels for students to repeat chorally.
4 Say each pair of vowels for individual students to repeat.
5 Write the pair of words on the board, in a column marked *1* or *2* (see the tables).
6 Say the vowel sound of one of the two words from the pair. Students must say *1* or *2*.
7 As you do more and more pairs, go back over the previous pairs until you are saying sounds from random from the whole set.

Put students into pairs to do the minimal pairs activity below. Each student says one word from each pair and the other tries to work out which. Point out that these are all English words, although the meanings are not important.

1	2
hard	had
heard	head
heed	hid
hoard	hod
who'd	hood
hoe	how
hey	hi

Exercise A

1 Check that students can identify each of the sectors from the pictures. Drill the pronunciation, particularly stress.
2 Set for pairwork. Elicit names from each sector until students run out. Encourage students to come up with more than one, but do not try to explain all jobs to all students.

Answers

1 1 Agriculture
   2 Manufacturing
   3 Finance
   4 Construction
   5 Leisure
   6 Retail
   7 Government
   8 Transport
2 Answers depend on the students. Note that in this case, *Government* equals *Public Sector*, so *doctor*, *nurse*, etc., would qualify because they could work in a state hospital. *Lawyer* and other professionals could work, clearly, in any sector.

Exercise B

Point out that students are going to hear the sounds of a particular job, or set of jobs. They do not have to name the job, only the employment sector. Play the first sound as an example. Play the remaining sounds.

Feed back, perhaps after each sound. You might like to get students to mime the actions they can hear to confirm their understanding.

Answers

The sounds are intended to indicate the following, but it does not matter if students do not always get it.

1 Construction
2 Agriculture
3 Manufacturing

4 Retail
5 Leisure
6 Transport
7 Finance
8 Government

Tapescript

Presenter: Lesson 3
            B Listen and say. Which sector are these people working in?
Sound effects: 1 erection of scaffolding
                2 the sound of a tractor
                3 machines working in the Manufacturing industry
                4 supermarket noises including bar code readers and tills
                5 people enjoying themselves at a swimming pool
                6 a heavy goods vehicle double-declutching
                7 a calculator with till roll advance
                8 the sounds of a hospital

Methodology note

Some of the sounds may be difficult to associate with a particular sector. This is not a problem as this is partly a game and partly a stimulus for language production. It does not matter whether the students get the answers 'right'.

Exercise C

Refer students to the flowchart. Remind them about the meaning of the diamond boxes – they contain *Yes/No* questions. Give students time to look carefully and see how the flowchart works.

1 Set for individual work and pairwork checking. Ask students to follow on the flowchart as they work through it. Play the conversation. Feed back.
2 Set for pairwork. Feed back, then drill the questions, making a point of the fall-rise at the main stressed syllable.

3   Get good students to ask you the three questions. Answer truthfully. Say whether you agree with the result. Set for pairwork. Monitor and assist.
4   General discussion. If students can see anything wrong with the design of the flowchart, and can explain how to make it better, good!

Answers
1   Leisure or Transport
2   The three questions are:
     • Would you like to work inside?
     • Would you like to meet new people (in your job)?
     • Would you like to travel?
3   Depend on the students.
4   Depend on the students.

Methodology note

Accept at this stage any reasonable way of pronouncing *Would you*. Students do not have to make the /dʒ/ sound, but they must not put in a vowel or a glottal.

Tapescript

Presenter: C 1 **Listen to Paul and Jane. They are talking about the flowchart. Which sector should Paul work in?**

Jane: What kind of job would you like to do after college, Paul?
Paul: I don't know, really.
Jane: There's a flowchart in this magazine to help you choose an employment sector.
Paul: Show me.
Jane: No, I want to see if it works. I'll ask you some questions, then I'll tell you the sector you should choose.
Paul: Right.
Jane: First question. Would you like to work inside?
Paul: Yes.

Jane: OK. Second question. Would you like to meet new people?
Paul: What? In my job?
Jane: Yes.
Paul: Yes, I would.
Jane: Right. Third question. Would you like to travel?
Paul: Yes, definitely.
Jane: OK. It says: The Leisure industry or the Transport industry. Do you agree with that?
Paul: Mmm. I'm not sure about the Transport industry, but the Leisure industry sounds good.

Closure

1   Say the stressed syllable of the target words from this lesson for students to identify and say, e.g.,
     /faɪ/ = *finance*
     /strʌk/ = *construction*
2   Flash magazine pictures of jobs from different sectors and get students to identify and say the sector.

Alternative closure

This is an alternative closure for monolingual classes. Ask students why they would like/not like to work in a particular sector. It is likely that very few, if any, of the students can do this well, so employ a Community Language Learning approach. This only really works if you speak the students' language well. Here is the idea:
1   You ask the question in English.
2   You allow the student to answer in their own language.
3   You work out how to give that answer in English.
4   You present it and drill it, with that student and the other students.
5   You ask the question again in English.
6   The student answers in English.

Lesson 4: Speaking

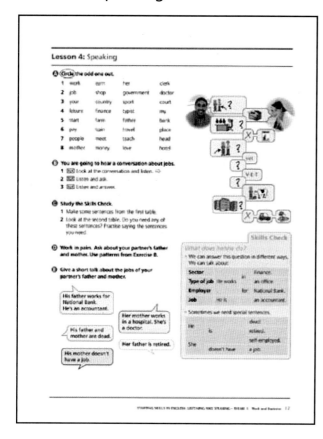

J	job
K	?
L	leisure
M	manager, manual, manufacturing, money
N	nurse
O	office
P	professional
Q	?
R	receptionist, retail
S	secretary
T	teacher, transport, typist
U	use
V	?
W	work, worker
X	?
Y	?
Z	?

Introduction

Write *The Alphabet Game* on the board. Elicit the alphabet, in the correct order and with good pronunciation of each letter. Ask students to try to think of a word connected with work and business beginning with each letter of the alphabet. Students should at least know and be able to say the following words.

Answers
Possible answers:

A	agriculture, architect
B	bank
C	clerk, computer, construction
D	doctor
E	employ, employment, engineer
F	farm, farmer, finance
G	government
H	hotel
I	industry

Exercise A

Refer students to the first row. Ask which is the odd one out. If students are struggling, say *Say each word.* If they still do not get it, say *Think about the vowel.* Elicit that *clerk* is the odd one out (in British English). Continue with the second row, and point out that this time, some of the words have more than one vowel sound. They must concentrate on the stressed vowel. Set for pairwork.

Feed back, drilling the three words with the same sound, then the odd one out in each case. Try to make sure that the majority of students can make a reasonable attempt at the sounds.

Answers

1	work	earn	her	*clerk*
2	job	shop	*government*	doctor
3	your	*country*	sport	court
4	*leisure*	finance	typist	my
5	start	farm	father	*bank*
6	pay	train	*travel*	place
7	people	meet	teach	*head*
8	mother	money	love	*hotel*

Exercise B

Refer students to the pictures. Remind them that the pictures will help them to remember the sentences in the conversation, but give them a few moments to look at the pictures and try to guess what some of the questions and answers might be.

1   Play the tape.
2   Get students going by giving them *What* as the start of the first question. Play the tape again, pausing after each answer for the next question.
3   Play the questions, pausing after each one for the students to answer.

Drill questions and answers from the conversation.

Tapescript

Presenter:	Lesson 4
	B 1 Look at the conversation and listen.
Man:	What does your father do?
Woman:	He works for National Bank.
Man:	Oh! Is he a manager?
Woman:	No, he's an accountant.
Man:	What about your mother?
Woman:	She's a vet.
Man:	A what?
Woman:	A vet. V-E-T.
Man:	What's that?
Woman:	It's a doctor for animals.
Man:	Does she work in an animal hospital?
Woman:	No. She travels a lot. She likes to work outside.

Presenter:	B 2 Listen and ask.
	[REPEAT OF EXERCISE B1]

Presenter:	B 3 Listen and answer.
	[REPEAT OF EXERCISE B1]

Exercise C

Refer students to the Skills Check.
1   Set for pairwork. Monitor and assist.
2   Explain as well as you can that sometimes you cannot answer the questions in the conversation with the sentences in the first table. Work through and, if appropriate, tell students about your situation – if one or both of your parents is retired, dead or self-employed, or without a job at the moment. Give students time individually to think which of these sentences they might need, and to practise saying them. Monitor and assist.

Exercise D

Set for pairwork. Monitor and assist. Allow students to take notes about the information they hear.

Exercise E

Refer students to the speech bubbles. Drill the sentences. Do the conversation with a good student, with you giving true information. Then get the good student to give a short talk about you. Ask a few more students to talk about their partners.

Closure

Make sure students can say all the target words from this theme with good pronunciation, particularly word stress and pronunciation of vowels.

General note

By the end of this theme, students should be able to hear and identify, in isolation and in context, the following words linked with science and nature. They should also be able to say them with reasonable pronunciation, especially stress in multi-syllable words, and use them in simple S V (O) (C) sentences.

dry	high	sea	wet
flower	light	strong	wind
fog	lightning	temperature	windy
foggy	low	thunderstorm	
forest	rain	water	
heavy	river	weather	

Lesson 1: Listening

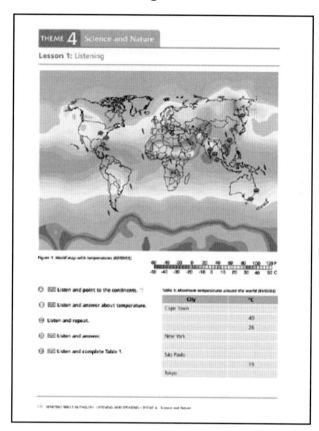

Introduction

Students may already be familiar with the following words from this lexical set:

cloud	island	snow
cold	map	sun
country	mountain	tree
hot	river	

They should also know basic colours. They have also met the word *continent*. If you are in any doubt, check that all the students can identify and produce these words in isolation.

1   Check or teach *hot* and *cold*.
2   Dictate geographic/natural features and get students to draw something. This should work for *mountain, river, island, trees, sun, cloud*.
3   Get students to name the colours in the order they appear in the scale underneath the temperature map. Allow them to call early colours *violet*, *purple* or *indigo*.

Then put some, or all, of the words into sentence context.

Exercise A

Refer students to the world map. Ask them what it shows. Push them to a full answer viz. *temperatures all over the world at 12 noon on July 2nd, 2005*. You may have to give them the word *temperatures*. Point out that for the rest of this lesson, they have to imagine this is the weather today around the world.

Explain to students that they are going to hear continent names. Tell them to point to the correct part of the map. Say or play the first word – *Africa* – as an example. Make sure all students are pointing to the correct place. Say or play the tape of the individual continents. Watch the students and try to identify any student who is not correctly associating the spoken word with the correct continent.

You can go through this activity several times, speeding up and saying words and individual sentences in a different order.

Tapescript

Presenter:		Theme 4 Science and Nature Lesson 1
		A Listen and point to the continents.
Voices:	1	Africa
	2	North America
	3	Asia
	4	Europe
	5	Antarctica
	6	Australia
	7	South America

Voices: 1 Have you ever been to Europe?
2 The Sahara Desert is in Africa.
3 Australia is the world's biggest island.
4 Is Turkey in Asia?
5 The continent in the south is called Antarctica.
6 Where's South America? Is it here?
7 Canada, Mexico and the USA are in North America.

Methodology note

Show students how to draw a quick sketch map of the world, based on simple geometric shapes. You could ask some students to come up and draw a map on the board.

Exercise B

Ask students what the colours mean. Elicit *different temperatures*. Ask them what *blue* means, etc. Say or play the first question: *What's the temperature in South Africa?* Continue with the remaining questions.

Answers
For the questions about temperature, accept approximate answers, or teach students to say *It's between ... and ...*

South America is about as hot as North America.

Students will struggle to answer the questions containing the superlative, but see what they can do.

For the last question, students may well need some help in finding their country on the map.

Tapescript

Presenter: B Listen and answer about temperature.

Voice: What's the temperature in South Africa?
What's the temperature in the UK?
What's the temperature in Antarctica?
What's the temperature in India?
Is North Africa hotter than South Africa?
Is Europe colder than North Africa?
Is it hotter at the Equator, or at the Poles?
Is South America hotter than North America?
Where is the hottest place?
Where is the coldest place?
What is the temperature in your country?

Methodology note

Where is the hottest/coldest place? requires students to understand the superlative, which has not yet been formally taught in this course. However, they should recognize the form from previous learning.

Exercise C

Draw some of the weather symbols from the map on the board. Say *rain* and *thunderstorm* as you draw the symbols. Then point to the rain symbol and say *It's raining*. Get students to repeat. Point to the symbol for thunderstorm and say *There's a thunderstorm*. Get students to repeat. Drill the two different structures.

You say: *rain*
Students say: *It's raining.*
You say: *thunderstorm*
Students say: *There's a thunderstorm.*

Add *hot, cold* with the structure *It's hot/cold*. Drill all four.

Exercise D

Revise *north, south, east, west*. Get students to point to parts of continents, e.g., East Africa, Southeast Asia, the west of Australia, the north of Europe.

Explain that they are going to hear questions about the weather in different parts of the world. Say or play the first one as an example. Do not let students shout out. Then elicit an answer and get other students to confirm or correct. Point out that we do not need *like* in the answer, e.g., *It's like raining*. Continue in the same way with the remaining questions.

Tapescript

Presenter: **D Listen and answer.**
Voice: 1 What's the weather like in the east of Australia?
   2 What's the weather like in the west of Africa?
   3 Is it raining in the east of Asia?
   4 Is there a thunderstorm in Europe?
   5 Are there thunderstorms in North America?
   6 Is it raining in Central Africa?

Language and culture notes

1 It is actually quite complex talking about the weather in English. There are three different structures:
  - *It's hot.* = It + be + adjective
  - *It's raining.* = It + present continuous
  - *There's a thunderstorm.* = There + be + a + noun

Students have to recognize which kind of word the weather feature is:
  - adjective: *hot, cold, warm, sunny*
  - verb: *snow, rain*
  - noun: *thunderstorm, thunder, lightning*

It does not sound very English, or it is plain wrong, to use the incorrect structure, e.g.,
  - *It's snowy.*
  - *It's sunning.*
  - *It's a thunderstorm.*

2 You may just be asked *What does it mean in these sentences?* Just say *It doesn't mean anything. We just say it in English, the same as we say 'It is eight o'clock.'*

Exercise E

Refer students to Table 1. Ask them what it shows. Point out that these are temperatures for the day before, i.e., yesterday (since they are imagining it is 2nd July!). Explain that they must listen and complete the table. Elicit the kind of information they must listen for – names and numbers (temperatures). Remind students that they must guess the spelling of names/proper nouns, then check later. Say or play the first two as examples. Set for individual work and pairwork checking. Continue with the remaining items. Give students time to compare answers/spellings. Feed back, building up the table on the board.

Answers

City	°C
Cape Town	16
Dubai	40
Mumbai	26
New York	27
Paris	20
São Paulo	25
Sydney	19
Tokyo	26

Tapescript

Presenter: E Listen and complete Table 1.

Voice: So what was the weather like yesterday? Let's look at some temperatures around the world. In Cape Town in South Africa, it was sixteen Celsius. That's sixteen, not sixty, of course. In Dubai, it was forty. That's forty, not fourteen. Very, very hot. Mumbai in India was twenty-six, while New York was a little hotter at twenty-seven. Paris was twenty, and São Paulo in Brazil, South America, was twenty-five. It was nineteen in Sydney in Australia, and a warm twenty-six in Tokyo in Japan.

Ask students about the weather in their cities (their hometowns and the one they are studying in) today and yesterday. Ask for a prediction for tomorrow, e.g., *What will the temperature be tomorrow?* Ask about other weather conditions: *Will it snow/rain? Will it be sunny? Will there be a thunderstorm?*

Closure

Make sure students can correctly stress, e.g., *14* vs *40*; *16* vs *60*.

Ask checking questions about the information in Table 1.

What was the temperature in Cape Town?
Which was hotter, São Paulo or Tokyo?
Was Cape Town colder than Paris?
Which two cities had the same temperature?

Lesson 2: Listening

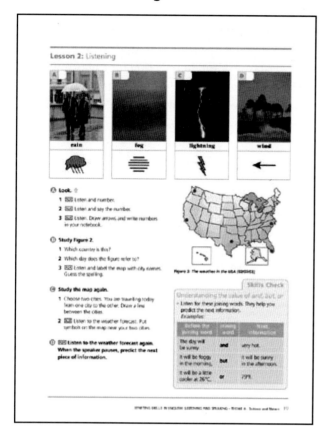

Introduction

Ask some questions about the weather in the maps and the table in Lesson 1. Ask about the weather today and yesterday in your present location and, if different, the students' hometown.

Exercise A

1   Refer students to the four pictures, but do not let them try to say the names of the types of weather condition. Set for individual work and pairwork checking. Play the tape. Students number the pictures. Feed back.
2   Tell students to listen again and say the number of the weather condition each time. They may hear about the same condition more than once. Feed back.
3   Explain that the arrow for wind shows the direction. This arrow means it is a west wind, or a

wind from the west. Point out also that we often write the speed, in miles per hour or kilometres per hour, on the arrow. So if we write *15* on this arrow, we mean there will be a wind from the west at fifteen miles per hour (or mph). Set for individual work and pairwork checking. Play the first one as an example. Make sure students are doing the correct thing. Continue with the remaining items. Feed back.

Answers

1   3 rain
    1 fog
    2 lightning
    4 wind
2   3 (rain)
    1 (fog)
    2 (lightning)
    4 (wind)
    3 (rain)
    1 (fog)
    4 (wind)
    2 (lightning)
3   1 $\xrightarrow{15}$
    2 $\xleftarrow{30}$
    3 $\uparrow$ 10
    4 $\downarrow$ 4
    5 $\nwarrow$ 40

Tapescript

Presenter: Lesson 2
            A 1 **Listen and number.**
    Voice: 1 fog
            2 lightning
            3 rain
            4 wind

Presenter: A 2 **Listen and say the number.**
    Voice: It's raining.
            It's foggy.
            Look at the lightning.
            It's so windy today.
            Look at the rain. It's absolutely pouring.

I can't see anything. This fog is so bad.
Listen to the wind in the trees.
I think a house has been hit by lightning.

Presenter: **A 3 Listen. Draw arrows and write numbers in your notebook.**

Voice:
1 There will be a wind from the west at fifteen miles per hour.
2 There will be a wind from the east at thirty miles per hour.
3 The wind will be from the south at ten miles per hour.
4 There will be a light north wind, four miles per hour.
5 The wind will be strong, southeasterly, forty miles per hour.

Exercise B

1 Refer students to the map. Ask the question chorally.
2 Elicit answers and confirm.
3 Refer students to the dots on the map. Elicit that they are cities. See if students can identify any of them. Do not confirm or correct. Set for individual work and pairwork checking. Play the tape. Point out that they may have to guess the spelling. Feed back. Confirm or correct the spelling. Check also that students can say where each city is, e.g., *Seattle is in the northwest.*

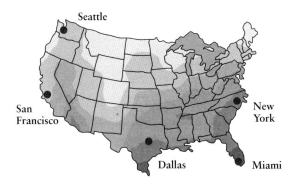

Tapescript

Presenter: **B 3 Listen and label the map with city names. Guess the spelling.**

Voice: Miami is in the southeast of the country. New York is in the northeast. Dallas is in the south. San Francisco is in the southwest, and Seattle is in the northwest.

Exercise C

1 Set for individual work. Make sure students have chosen two cities. Point out that they only have to listen for the forecast for those cities.
2 Play the tape.
Feed back, ideally onto an OHT of the figure on which you can draw weather symbols.

Answers

	°C/F	Wind direction and speed (mph/kph)	Lightning	Other
Seattle	14/57	S – 8/13	✗	light rain
San Francisco	13/55	E – 5/8	✗	fog, sunny
Dallas	35/95	N – 30/43	✓	sunny, hot, heavy rain, thunderstorms
Miami	26/79	SW 10/16	✓	heavy rain, thunderstorms
New York	22/72	NW 4/6	✗	sunny, warm

Methodology note

This is mainly a listening lesson, so do not worry if the pronunciation of words is not particularly good. Also do not insist on full sentences. Students will get more practice in the next lesson.

Tapescript

Presenter: C 2 **Listen to the weather forecast. Put symbols on the map near your two cities.**

Weatherman: And now here's the weather forecast for the 2nd July, 2005. Firstly, let's look at the northwest. The temperature in Seattle will be fourteen degrees Celsius, which is fifty-seven degrees Fahrenheit, with a wind from the south at eight miles, or thirteen kilometres, per hour. There will be light rain in the afternoon.

Further south, in San Francisco, it will be cooler at thirteen degrees Celsius, or fifty-five degrees Fahrenheit, with a light east wind of five miles per hour, or eight kilometres per hour. It will be foggy in the morning, but it will be sunny in the afternoon.

Moving to the east, in the morning Dallas will be sunny and very hot, thirty-five degrees, that's ninety-five degrees Fahrenheit, but there will be a strong thirty-mile-per-hour, or forty-three-kilometre-per-hour, wind from the north, and that will bring heavy rain and thunderstorms in the afternoon.

Further east, in Miami, it will be a little cooler, at twenty-six degrees Celsius, or seventy-nine degrees Fahrenheit, but there will be heavy rain here too, and thunderstorms. The wind will be from the southeast, I mean the southwest, at ten miles per hour, or sixteen kilometres per hour.

Finally, New York. The day will be sunny and warm at twenty-two degrees Celsius, seventy-two degrees Fahrenheit, and there will be a light wind from the northwest, perhaps four miles per hour – that's just six kilometres per hour. And that's your weather forecast. Have a nice day!

Exercise D

Refer students to the Skills Check. Point out that the joining words help you to predict the kind of information coming next, even if you cannot give the exact information. Set for individual work. Play the tape. Do not let students shout out at the pauses. Give everyone time to think, then elicit a few answers before allowing the tape to continue.

Tapescript

Presenter: D **Listen to the weather forecast again. When the speaker pauses, predict the next piece of information.**
[REPEAT OF EXERCISE C2]

Methodology note

We do not normally allow students to listen to the same passage more than once since this is not normally possible in real life, but this is listening for a technical purpose and, therefore, arguably a second listening is reasonable.

Closure

Ask students to predict the next word in these cases:

The wind will be very (strong).
The sun will be very (hot).
The rain will be very (heavy).
It is raining very (hard).
The fog will be very (thick). This is a new collocation, but some students may know it.
The day will be warm, but the night will be very (cold).
It will be hot, but there will be some light (rain).
Tomorrow, the weather will be much (worse/better).

Ask students to predict the weather for tomorrow.

Lesson 3: Speaking

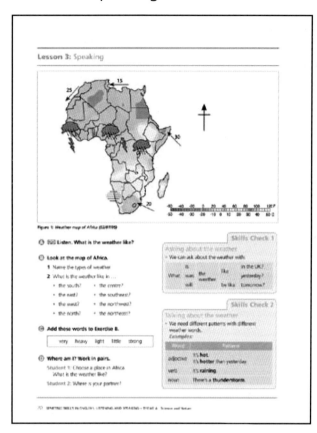

Introduction

Revise the main vowel sounds with words connected with science and nature.

long vs short
(based on the stressed syllable in each case)

1	2
hard	map
worse	heavy
	weather
	temperature
	west
tree	wind
east	river

1	2
north	fog
or	hot
(warm)	cold
(cool)	continent
	sun
	country

( ) = not formally presented in this course

diphthongs

1	2
snow	mountain
	cloud
	south
rain	light
	lightning
	island

Follow this procedure in each case.

1 Say a word from each pair several times, e.g., *hard – map.* Do not let students say anything.
2 Isolate the vowel sounds. Do not let students say anything.
3 Say each pair of stressed vowels for students to repeat chorally.
4 Say each pair of vowels for individual students to repeat.
5 Write the pair of words on the board, in a column marked *1* or *2* (see the tables).
6 Say the vowel sound of one of the two words from the pair. Students must say *1* or *2*.
7 As you do more and more pairs, go back over the previous pairs until you are saying sounds from random from the whole set.

Put students into pairs to do the minimal pairs activity below. Each student says one word from each pair and the other tries to work out which. Point out that these are all English words, although the meanings are not important.

1	2
can't	can
curve	Kev
keen	kin
cord	cod
cooed	could
coe	cow
cray	cry

Language and culture note

At first sight, you may be surprised to see *cool* as a /uː/ word. In fact, the vowel **is** /uː/, but the final (dark) *l* changes the vowel quality.

Exercise A

Explain to students that they are going to hear the sound of weather! If students find the idea funny, that is fine. They must identify and say the kind of weather, but they must not shout out. They must wait until they are invited to speak. Play the first sound as an example. If they give you *rain*, ask for more details. Elicit *light rain*. Continue with the remaining sounds. Feed back.

Refer students to Skills Check 1 and drill the questions. Remind or teach students not to use *like* in the answers.

Answers
Model answers:

1   light rain
2   heavy rain
3   light wind
4   strong wind
5   thunderstorm
6   fog
7   snow

Tapescript
Presenter:	Lesson 3
	A Listen. What is the weather like?
Sound effects:	1 light rain
	2 heavy rain
	3 light wind
	4 strong wind
	5 a thunderstorm
	6 a foghorn
	7 snow

Exercise B

Refer students to Figure 1. Ask them if they can identify any of the countries. Confirm or correct, or give them an atlas to check their ideas.
1   Put students in pairs to talk about the kinds of weather in different parts of the continent.
2   Move students on to this exercise.
For these exercises, allow students to use single words or phrases, rather than full sentences. Feed back. As you do so, turn single words and short phrases into full sentences.

Exercise C

Refer students to Skills Check 2. Drill the three patterns. Give examples of weather words and get students to identify the part of speech in each case, e.g.,
>   *hot – adjective*
>   *cold – adjective*
>   *thunderstorm – noun*
>   *lightning – noun*
>   *rain – verb/noun*
>   *snow – verb/noun*, etc.

Move into a pattern drill, e.g.,

You say:	*hot*
Students say:	*It is hot.*
You say:	*rain* (verb)
Students say:	*It is raining.*
You say:	*lightning*
Students say:	*There is lightning.*

Refer students to the extra words to describe different weather conditions, e.g.,
>   *very = It's very hot / cold / sunny.*
>   *light/heavy = There is light/heavy rain.*
>   *light/strong = There is a light/strong wind.*
>   *little = It's a little hotter/colder today.*

Teach students to say also:
>   *There's no rain./It isn't raining.*
>   *There's no wind./It isn't windy.*

Exercise D

Put students into pairs. Demonstrate how to do the exercise. Remind students about the use of *and/but*, and encourage them to use the words in their weather descriptions. Monitor and assist. Ask a few pairs to do the exercise for the other students.

Closure

Say the stressed syllable of the target words from this lesson for students to identify and say as follows:

/he/ = *heavy*
/temp/ = *temperature*
/kɒn/ = *continent*
/kʌn/ = *country*
/we/ = *weather*
/laɪt/ = *light* or *lightning*
/lɪt/ = *little*

Lesson 4: Speaking

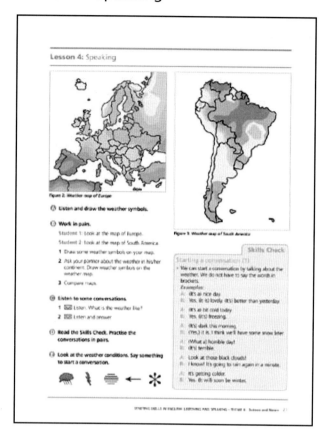

Introduction

Refer students to the two maps. Elicit the names of countries from the continents. See if any students can actually locate individual countries on the maps. Students should at least be able to find Brazil in South America, and Spain, France and Italy in Europe.

Exercise A

Dictate weather conditions, including speed with winds. Use a variety of structures from the theme to date, e.g.,

The rain is very heavy.
It's foggy.
There's a thunderstorm.
There is a wind of fifteen miles per hour from the east.

Add *snow*, e.g., *It's snowing.*

Answers

1 heavy rain – a cloud with several oblique raindrops
2 fog – vertical lines
3 a thunderstorm – a cloud with several oblique raindrops and a lightning flash
4 a wind arrow from west to east, with the number 15 on it to show speed
5 a snowflake

Exercise B

Set for pairwork. Make sure students understand the task, especially that they must not show their completed map to their partner until the end of the activity. Encourage students to use full sentences and a range of patterns, plus *and/but*. Monitor and assist. Feed back. Deal with any common difficulties you noticed.

Exercise C

Make some 'phatic communion' sentences without warning, e.g.,

Nice day, isn't it?
Better than yesterday.
Hope it stays fine.
Bit wet today.
Cold for the time of year.

Point out that people often use the weather to start a conversation.

1 Play the tape. Ask after each section: *What's the weather like?* If relevant, ask *What was the weather like yesterday? What will it be like later/tomorrow?*
2 Play the tape again. Stop after each pause for students to answer.

Tapescript

Presenter: Lesson 4

C 1 **Listen. What is the weather like?**

Voice 1: Nice day.

Voice 2: Yes, lovely. Better than yesterday.
[PAUSE]

Voice 3: Bit cold today.

Voice 4: Yes, freezing.
[PAUSE]

Voice 1: Dark this morning.

Voice 2: It is. I think we'll have some snow later.
[PAUSE]

Voice 3: Horrible day!

Voice 4: Terrible!
[PAUSE]

Voice 1: Look at those black clouds!

Voice 2: I know! It's going to rain again in a minute.
[PAUSE]

Voice 3: It's getting colder.

Voice 4: Yes. Soon be winter.

Presenter: C 2 **Listen and answer.**

Voice 1: Nice day.
[PAUSE]

Voice 3: Bit cold today.
[PAUSE]

Voice 1: Dark this morning.
[PAUSE]

Voice 3: Horrible day!
[PAUSE]

Voice 1: Look at those black clouds!
[PAUSE]

Voice 3: It's getting colder.

Exercise D

Refer students to the Skills Check. Work through the conversations, showing the ellipsis. Dictate some of the elliptical sentences and elicit the full version, e.g.,

You say: *Nice day.*
Students say: *It's a nice day.*

Set for pairwork.

Exercise E

Continue the pairwork. Get students to respond in each case.

Closure

Make sure students can say all the target words from this theme with good pronunciation, particularly word stress and pronunciation of vowels.

General note

By the end of this theme, students should be able to hear and identify, in isolation and in context, the following words linked with the physical world. They should also be able to say them with reasonable pronunciation, especially stress in multi-syllable words, and use them in simple S V (O) (C) sentences.

above	between	in the centre of	opposite
behind	corner	near	out (of an area)
below	in front of	next to	

Lesson 1: Listening

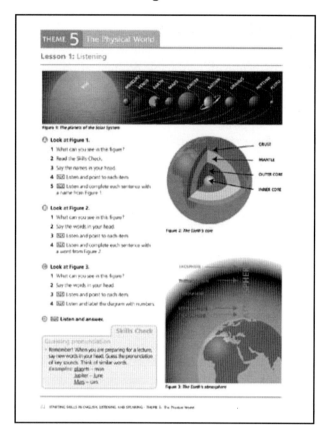

Introduction

Students may already be familiar with the following words from this lexical set:

bottom	mountain
centre	north
coast	right
country	river
east	south
island	top
lake	town
left	village
map	west

They should also know basic colours. They have also met the word *continent*. If you are in any doubt, check that all the students can identify and produce these words in isolation.

1 Check or teach the opposites/converses, i.e., *top/bottom, left/right, east/west, north/south*.

2 Dictate geographic/natural features and get students to draw something. This should work for *mountain, river, island, lake, coast*.

3 Get students to name the colours in rainbow/spectrum order. Allow them to call early colours *violet, purple* or *indigo*.

4 Elicit the names of the continents.

Then put some, or all, of the words into sentence context.

Exercise A

Ask students how many figures they can see on the page. (There are three.) Refer them to the first figure.

1 Do as a whole-class, high-speed activity.

2 Set as individual work.

3 Set as individual work.

4 Play the first item as an example. Continue with the rest. Students can work in pairs and check each other's choices.

5 Play the first item as an example. Remind students not to shout out. After holding the students for a few seconds in each case, allow them to offer ideas, then play the remainder of the item.

Tapescript

Presenter:	Theme 5 The Physical World
	Lesson 1
	A 4 Listen and point to each item.
Voice:	planets
	Jupiter
	Mars
	Mercury
	Neptune
	Pluto
	Saturn
	the Earth

the Sun
Uranus
Venus

Presenter: **A 5** **Listen and complete each sentence with a name from Figure 1.**

Voices:
1 At the centre of the Solar System is [PAUSE] the Sun.
2 The nearest planet to the Sun is called [PAUSE] Mercury.
3 The fourth planet from the Sun is called [PAUSE] Mars.
4 There is a large planet with rings. It is called [PAUSE] Saturn.
5 The largest planet in our Solar System is [PAUSE] Jupiter.
6 The planet between Pluto and Uranus is called [PAUSE] Neptune.
7 The planet next to Mercury is called [PAUSE] Venus.
8 The smallest planet and the furthest planet from the Sun is called [PAUSE] Pluto.

Methodology notes

1 You ask yourself, while doing the exercises on this page, why you are teaching students the planets, the layers of the Earth's core and the layers of the atmosphere. Surely these words are far too complex for this level? That is true, which is why the target of the lesson is **not** to learn these words as such, but rather to associate the sound of each word with the spelling of the word. This is a key skill in English with proper nouns especially, to pick them out in the stream of speech and to hear the prepositions of place prior to learning how to use them to describe location. It is this last set, the prepositions of place, which are the key learning items for this theme.

2 Having said that, the information contained in Figure 2 is useful background to the lesson on continental drift.

3 Point out the basic patterns of sound-sight in the stressed syllables of words in this lesson. Students should be able to use these patterns to predict the sounds of the words, i.e.,

Sound	Examples	Notes
/æ/	Sa(turn) man(tle) stra(tosphere)	
/e/	Nep(tune) me(sosphere) ex(osphere)	
/ʌ/	crust	
/ɒ/	tro(posphere)	
/ɜː/	Mer(cury) ther(mosphere)	
/ɒː/	Mars	
/ɔː/	core	
/ju/	U(ranus)	common sound of *u*
/uː/	Plu(to) Ju(piter)	another common sound of *u*

There is one clear exception: *Venus* is not /venuːs/.

Exercise B

Repeat the procedure from Exercise A.

Tapescript

Presenter: B 3 Listen and point to each item.
Voice: the Earth
the crust
the inner core
the mantle
the outer core

Presenter: B 4 Listen and complete each sentence with a word from Figure 2.
Voices: The top part of the Earth is called [PAUSE] the crust.
The centre of the Earth is called [PAUSE] the inner core.
Next to the inner core is the [PAUSE] outer core.
Between the crust and the outer core, there is a layer called [PAUSE] the mantle.
The mantle is above the [PAUSE] outer core.
The mantle is below the [PAUSE] crust.

Exercise C

Repeat the procedure from Exercise A.

Answers

1 troposphere – 10 km
2 stratosphere – 40 km
3 mesosphere – 50 km
4 thermosphere – 300 km
5 exosphere – 400 km

Tapescript

Presenter: C 3 Listen and point to each item.
Voice: the atmosphere
the exosphere
the mesosphere
the stratosphere
the thermosphere
the troposphere

Presenter: C 4 Listen and label the diagram with numbers.
Voice: There are five layers in the atmosphere. The lowest layer is called the troposphere. This is the weather layer with clouds. The troposphere goes up to ten kilometres. The stratosphere is above the troposphere. This layer is forty kilometres high. The next layer is the mesosphere. This layer is fifty kilometres high. The mesosphere is below the thermosphere. This layer occupies the next three hundred kilometres. Finally, above the thermosphere is the exosphere. This layer goes up another four hundred kilometres.

Exercise D

Check or teach the word *layer*, which has been used already, but not focused on. Set for pairwork. Feed back, eliciting answers from several pairs before confirming or correcting. Do not worry if the pronunciation of the nouns is not good. That is not the target of this lesson, as pointed out previously. However, if students are getting something factually wrong, it is probably because they are not making the correct semantic connection between a preposition of place and/or sound-sight of a noun from the figures. Go over these carefully.

Answers

1 Mercury
2 Mars
3 Jupiter
4 the inner core
5 the mantle
6 the outer core
7 the exosphere
8 the troposphere
9 300 kilometres
10 the mesosphere

Tapescript

Presenter: D Listen and answer.

Voices: 1 Which is the nearest planet to the Sun?
2 Which planet is between the Earth and Jupiter?
3 Which is the largest planet in the Solar System?
4 What is the inner part of the Earth called?
5 Which layer is between the crust and the outer core?
6 Which layer is below the mantle?
7 What is the outer layer of the atmosphere called?
8 What is the weather layer of the atmosphere called?
9 How high is the thermosphere?
10 What is above the stratosphere?

Closure

Ask students to close their books and try to draw one, or all, of the three figures. They must label them, but only with the first letter of each item.

Lesson 2: Listening

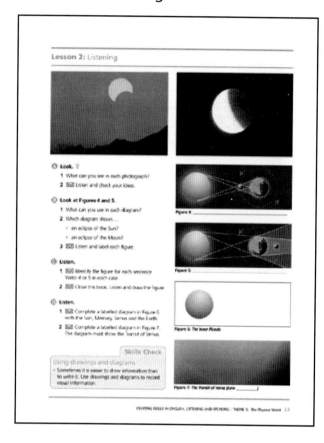

eclipse of the Sun. Eclipses of the Sun happen every eighteen months somewhere on the Earth, but total eclipses only happen once every one hundred years on average. A total eclipse happens when the Moon completely covers the Sun. In a partial eclipse, the Moon does not move exactly between the Earth and the Sun.

Presenter: **Part 2**
Voice: The picture on the right shows the Moon. The Earth is moving between the Sun and the Moon. This is an eclipse of the Moon. On average, three eclipses of the Moon happen every year somewhere on the Earth. Total eclipses happen nearly as often as partial eclipses.

Introduction

Ask the questions again from Exercise D of Lesson 1.

Exercise A

1   Refer students to the pictures. Set for pairwork. Elicit some ideas, but do not confirm or correct.
2   Play each part in turn. Then say each script, pausing for students to complete correctly, e.g., *The photograph on the left shows … the Sun.*, etc.

Tapescript

Presenter: Lesson 2
A 2 **Listen and check your ideas.**
Part 1
Voice: The picture on the left shows the Sun. We can see a shadow on it. The Moon is moving between the Earth and the Sun. This is an

Methodology note

The word *eclipse* is not an item of target vocabulary, but it must be clearly understood for this lesson. However, it is relatively hard to say, so do not worry if students cannot pronounce it correctly.

Exercise B

1   Refer students to Figures 4 and 5. Set for pairwork. Elicit some ideas, but do not confirm or correct.
2   Repeat the procedure.
3   Play the tape, then say each script, pausing for students to complete correctly, e.g., *In Figure 4, you can see the Moon between … the Earth and the Sun.*, etc.

Tapescript

Presenter: B 3 Listen and label each figure.

Voice: In Figure 4, you can see the Moon between the Earth and the Sun. This is an eclipse of the Sun. In Figure 5, you can see the Earth between the Moon and the Sun. This is an eclipse of the Moon.

Exercise C

1 Explain that students are going to hear some sentences. They must write the number of the sentence, then the number of the figure, e.g., *1 4*. Play the first one as an example and make sure everyone knows what they are doing. Play the remaining sentences. Feed back orally.

2 Explain that this time they must draw a figure. Play the tape. Feed back, getting students to tell you what to draw on the board. Do what they say, even if it was quite wrong. Get other students to correct.

Answers

1 4
2 5
3 4
4 4
5 5
6 5
7 5

Students should draw an eclipse of the Moon, i.e., like Figure 5.

Tapescript

Presenter: C 1 Identify the figure for each sentence. Write *4* or *5* in each case.

Voice: 1 The diagram shows an eclipse of the Sun.

2 The diagram shows an eclipse of the Moon.

3 The Moon is between the Earth and the Sun.

4 The Moon is in front of the Sun.

5 The Moon is behind the Earth.

6 The Earth is between the Sun and the Moon.

7 The Earth is in front of the Moon.

Presenter: C 2 Close this book. Listen and draw the figure.

Voice: The Moon goes round the Earth. The Earth goes round the Sun. Sometimes, the Earth is between the Moon and the Sun. We call this an eclipse of the Moon.

Exercise D

1 Refer students to the box marked Figure 6. Explain that they must draw a diagram in this box from the information they hear. They must label it correctly. Play Part 1. Feed back, drawing the diagram on the board as per their instructions, as before.

2 Refer students to the box marked Figure 7. Explain that they must draw a diagram in this box from the information they hear. They must label it correctly. Play Part 2. Feed back, drawing the diagram on the board as per their instructions, as before.

Answers

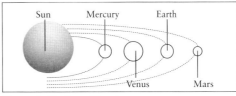

Figure 6: *The Inner Planets*

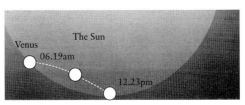

Figure 7: *The Transit of Venus (June 8th, 2004)*

Tapescript

Presenter: **D 1 Complete a labelled diagram in Figure 6 with the Sun, Mercury, Venus and the Earth.**

Voice: Mercury is the nearest planet to the Sun. Venus is next to Mercury. The Earth is the third planet from the Sun. In other words, Mercury and Venus are nearer the Sun than the Earth. Mars is next to the Earth. These planets are called The Inner Planets. Sometimes Mercury or Venus moves between the Earth and the Sun.

Presenter: **D 2 Complete a labelled diagram in Figure 7. The diagram must show the Transit of Venus.**

Voice: On 8th June, 2004, people in Europe, Asia and Africa watched a black circle move across the Sun. It moved from left to right across the bottom left corner of the Sun. The black circle was the planet Venus. When Mercury or Venus moves between the Earth and the Sun, we call it a transit, not an eclipse. The Transit of Venus in June 2004 started at 6.19 a.m. and ended at 12.23 p.m. In other words, it lasted just over six hours. Transits of Venus do not happen very often. There have only been six since 1608 and we will not see the next one in the UK until 2247.

Closure

1 Refer students to the Skills Check. Work through the information.
2 Say the stressed syllables from some of the words in this lesson and the last one. See if students can point to the item on the double page spread, e.g., *Mer, Ju, Sat.*

Lesson 3: Speaking

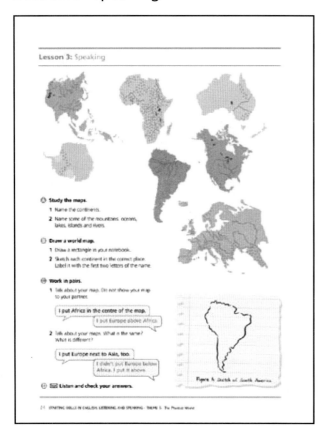

diphthongs

1	2
near	where
	there
coast	south
below	town
	mountain
behind	lake
right	
island	

Follow this procedure in each case.

1   Say a word from each pair several times, e.g., *Mars – Saturn*. Do not let students say anything.
2   Isolate the vowel sounds. Do not let students say anything.
3   Say each pair of stressed vowels for students to repeat chorally.
4   Say each pair of vowels for individual students to repeat.
5   Write the pair of words on the board, in a column marked *1* or *2* (see the tables).
6   Say the vowel sound of one of the two words from the pair. Students must say *1* or *2*.
7   As you do more and more pairs, go back over the previous pairs until you are saying sounds from random from the whole set.

Introduction

Revise the main vowel sounds with words connected with the physical world.

long vs short
(based on the stressed syllable in each case)

1	2
Mars	mantle
	map
	Saturn
between	in
east	river
Venus	sea
	village
corner	top
north	
core	

1	2
Pluto	front
Jupiter	country
	above
	Sun
Mercury	next
Earth	west
	left
	centre

Put students into pairs to do the minimal pairs activity below. Each student says one word from each pair and the other tries to work out which. Point out that these are all English words, although the meanings are not important.

1	2
barn	ban
burn	Ben
bean	bin
born	Bonn
bow*	bow*
bay	buy

*homographs with different pronunciations

Exercise A

1   Set for pairwork. Monitor and assist. Feed back
    orally. Ask some quick questions using the target
    vocabulary – *above, below, next to, top left,
    bottom right* – then get students to tell you where
    each continent is on the page, using prepositions of
    place.
2   This activity probably works best in a multicultural
    group. If all students come from one area, they
    may only be able to name items in that area. Set
    for pairwork. Feed back orally.

Methodology notes

1   It does not matter how many, if any, of the
    items on these maps can be named by the
    students. The fact that they are talking about
    the physical features is the important point.
2   The word *ocean* has not been formally
    presented, but should be known by now. It is
    needed for these lessons.

Answers
From left to right:

Asia	Africa	Australia
Antarctica	S. America	N. America
		Europe

Exercise B

Ask students to draw a quick sketch map of the world,
using triangles and rectangles. (See the Answers for
Exercise D.) Set for individual work. Point out that
they must not show their map to anybody. Monitor,
but do not confirm or correct.

Answers
After Exercise D.

Exercise C

1   Work through the first set of speech bubbles. Drill
    the sentences. Check pronunciation of the target
    words, i.e., *above, below, between, next to, in the
    centre of, on the left/right*. Set for pairwork. Do
    not confirm or correct.
2   Work through the second set of speech bubbles.
    Drill the sentences. Check pronunciation of the
    target words again. Set for pairwork. Do not
    confirm or correct.

Exercise D

Explain that students are now going to hear the correct
place for each continent. Play the tape. Feed back,
building up the map on the board. Follow the students'
instructions, then get other students to correct them.

Answers

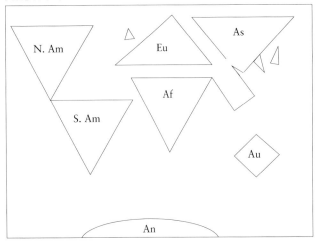

Tapescript

Presenter: Lesson 3

D Listen and check your answers.

Voice: In the west, there are two continents, North America and South America. North America is, of course, above South America. In the centre of the map is Africa. Above Africa is Europe. Asia is next to Africa. Australia is in the bottom right corner. Antarctica is in the south, in the middle.

Closure

1   Get students to close their notebooks. Give a cut-up version of the sketch map on page 85 to students so they can physically move the continents into the correct positions, then make a sketch map.

2   Get students to describe their map, using the target prepositions of place.

Lesson 4: Speaking

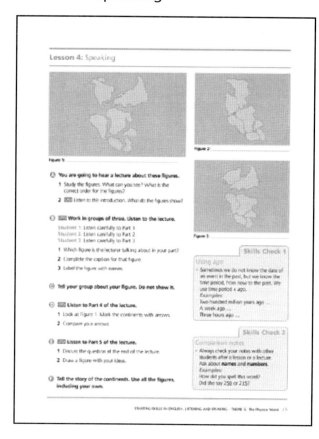

L   *lake*
M   *mantle, Mars, Mercury, Moon, mountain*
N   *Neptune, north*
O   *ocean*
P   *planet, Pluto*
Q   ?
R   *river*
S   *Saturn, sea, south, Sun*
T   *tree*
U   *Uranus*
V   *Venus*
W   *west, world*
X   ?
Y   ?
Z   ?

Note that many of these words have not been formally presented, but students may know them.

Introduction

Play *The Alphabet Game* with words connected with Space and the physical world. Ask students to try to think of at least one word beginning with each letter of the alphabet. Give clues, including mime and drawings.

Answers
Possible answers:

A   *Africa, Antarctica, Asia, atmosphere, Australia*
B   *bay*
C   *cloud, coast, continent, core, country, crust*
D   *desert*
E   *Earth, east*
F   *forest*
G   *geography, geology*
H   ?
I   *island*
J   *Jupiter*
K   ?

Exercise A

1   Refer students to the figures. It would be nice to think that they can identify the continents from their prior learning but, of course, they may not be able to. It does not matter. Do not confirm or correct their ideas. Ask the second question, but once again, do not confirm or correct.
2   Set for individual work and pairwork checking. Play the introduction.

Feed back, eliciting what the drawings show and the time in the past we are talking about. Draw a timeline on the board. Show the present, then show 250 million years ago, i.e., an arrow pointing backwards.

Answers
These drawings show the continents at various points in history/pre-history. It is not possible to say exactly the correct order, and you certainly should not confirm or correct.

Tapescript

Presenter: Lesson 4
A 2 Listen to the introduction.
What do the figures show?
Introduction

Lecturer: Today I am going to talk to you about the history of the Earth. I am going to start more than two hundred and fifty million years ago. What did the Earth look like at that time? According to scientists, it looked very different from the way it looks today. The animals were different of course, but the continents were different, too.

Methodology note

This is a speaking lesson, but there is a lot of listening in it. There is a simple explanation. Students need to have something to speak about and, ideally, the content should be relatively controlled so the teacher knows what the student will say and how to work with it to improve it. The best way to build this information is through listening, as the medium of communication is the same – spoken language.

Exercise B

Set for groupwork. Make sure students understand what they have to do. Play Parts 1, 2 and 3. Do not feed back.

Answers
After Exercise C.

Tapescript

Presenter: B Listen to the lecture.
Part 1

Lecturer: Two hundred and fifty million years ago, there was only one continent. Scientists called it Pangea. The word *Pangea* means 'all lands'. This continent went from the north to the south. Around the continent, there was one ocean, called Panthalassa. This word, of course, means 'all seas'.

Presenter: **Part 2**

Lecturer: What happened to Pangea? About two hundred million years ago, a split appeared, and Pangea became two continents. Scientists called the continent in the Northern Hemisphere Laurasia, and the continent in the Southern Hemisphere Gondwanaland. The present continents of Europe, North America and Asia were in Laurasia, and South America, Africa, Australia and Antarctica were in Gondwanaland. The subcontinent of India was also in Gondwanaland.

Presenter: **Part 3**

Lecturer: What happened to Laurasia and Gondwanaland? Eighty-five million years ago, splits appeared in both continents. Laurasia became two continents – North America and Europe with Asia. Gondwanaland became five continents – Antarctica, Australia, South America, Africa and India. Arabia began to split from Africa.

Methodology notes

1 This is the first time this exercise has been done. Make sure students realize that they only have to listen carefully to one part. Although this is set up artificially here, there is some basis in reality for this kind of activity. We sometimes tune out until there is a piece of information that is interesting to us, then we focus on it.

2 Students should be getting reasonably good at guessing spelling of proper nouns from the sound. In these cases, all the spellings are predictable. Check the spelling and point out where the wrong sound-sight relationship has been made.

Exercise C

Set for groupwork. Monitor and assist. Feed back, ensuring that students have got the information in the Answers below. Refer students to Skills Check 1 and Skills Check 2. Then work through the points.

Answers

1   Part 1: Figure 2
     Part 2: Figure 3
     Part 3: Figure 1
2   Figure 1: 85 million years ago
     Figure 2: 250 million years ago
     Figure 3: 200 million years ago
3   Figure 1

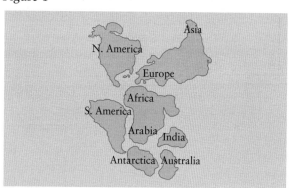

Figure 2

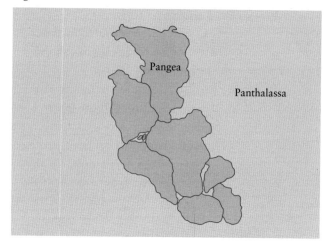

Figure 3

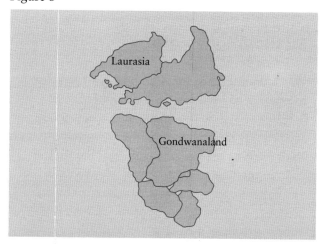

Exercise D

Set for individual work and pairwork checking. Feed back orally. Get students to tell you how the arrows should go on Figure 1. Highlight the basic prepositions of movement – *away from/towards*. Ensure that students understand the meaning.

Answers

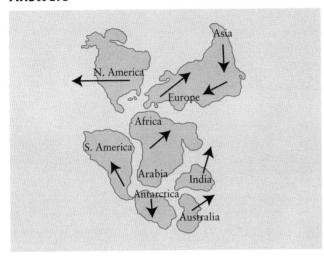

Tapescript

Presenter: D Listen to Part 4 of the lecture.
Part 4

Lecturer: For the next fifty million years, the continents kept moving. North America moved away from Europe and Asia. It moved to the west. South America moved away from Africa to the northwest. Antarctica moved to the south. Africa, India and Australia moved to the northeast. India kept moving towards Asia. Finally, India crashed into Asia. What happened? The huge Himalayan Mountains appeared with the highest mountain in the world, Mount Everest.

Exercise E

Set for pairwork. Feed back, getting drawings on the board.

Answers
Depend on the students.

Tapescript

Presenter: E Listen to Part 5 of the lecture.
Part 5

Lecturer: The continents are still moving today. What will the world look like in fifty million years' time?

Exercise F

This can be done as a whole-class activity, with students helping each other and contributing to the story as a whole, or in small groups.

Closure

Make sure students understand and can produce all the key words from this theme, with good pronunciation and stress.

Language and culture note

Students may wonder how we know about continental drift. We know it because scientists have found fossils of the same kind of animals all over the world. These animals could not swim. Therefore, at one time, there was no Pacific Ocean between Asia and the Americas, for example. Bits of continents also fit together, like a jigsaw.

THEME 6 Culture and Civilization

General note

By the end of this theme, students should be able to hear and identify, in isolation and in context, the following words linked with culture and civilization. They should also be able to say them with reasonable pronunciation, especially stress in multi-syllable words, and use them in simple S V (O) (C) sentences.

age	die	married	thank
born	family	party	thank you
congratulations	group	present (*n*)	
dead	guest	single	

In the listening activities in Lesson 1, there are three structure points which have not been formally dealt with to date:

1 Saxon genitive, e.g., *the man's family*
2 Ditransitive verbs, e.g., *giving the woman a ring*
3 *Everbody* + singular verb but plural pronoun, e.g., *Everybody dies, don't they?*

These are for comprehension only at this stage. They are analyzed and practised later.

Lesson 1: Listening

Introduction

Students may already be familiar with the following words from this lexical set:

adult	male
baby	man/men
boy	old
child/children	people/person
female	teenager
friend	woman/women
girl	young

If you are in any doubt, check that all the students can identify and produce these words in isolation.

1   Check or teach the opposites/converses, i.e., *adult/child; man/woman*, etc.
2   Say words with irregular plurals and ask students if the word is singular or plural.
3   Ask students to say life periods in order, beginning with *baby*.
4   Ask students for female words, then male words.

Then put some, or all, of the words into sentence context.

Remind or tell students that the word *teenager* means the period between the ages of 13 and 19, because all the numbers end in *teen*.

Exercise A

Give students plenty of time to look at all three pictures before eliciting any answers.

Answer

Model answer:

The three pictures show important events from the life of one person – birth, marriage and death.

Methodology note

This is a deep-end strategy activity. Students may be able to say a lot with good structure and pronunciation, or they may only be able to say isolated words. Do not correct. Confirm anything that is reasonable. By the end of the lesson, they should be able to do much better.

Exercise B

Refer students to the first picture.

1   Set for individual work and pairwork checking. Play the tape. Students may already know these words from their previous learning.
2   Demonstrate that students must answer with a full short answer, i.e., *Yes, it is./No, they aren't.* Play the first word as an example. Continue with the remainder. Remember to allow all students time to think of the answer before nominating someone to reply.
3   Play the tape. Students must give information in their replies.

4   Refer students to the Skills Check. Work through the points. Then play the tape.

Tapescript

Presenter: Theme 6 Culture and Civilization
             Lesson 1
             B 1 Listen and find.
Voice: a baby
             a boy
             a girl
             a man
             a woman
             an adult
             a child
             a teenager
             a present
             a guest

Presenter: **B 2 Listen. Say *Yes* or *No*.**
Voice: Is this a party?
             Is it a birthday party?
             Is the baby one today?
             Is the teenager giving the baby a present?
             Is it a big present?
             Are the people happy?
             Are they laughing?
             Is the baby happy?
             Is the baby laughing?

Presenter: **B 3 Listen. Give information.**
Voice: What is the teenager doing?
             What is the baby doing?
             How old is the baby?
             How many people are at the party?
             Who is giving the present?
             Who is taking the present?

Presenter: **B 4 Listen. Say *Yes*, *No*, or give information.**
Voice: Are the people laughing?
             How many people are at the party?
             How old is the baby?
             Are the people happy?

Is it a birthday party?
What is the teenager doing?
Is the baby laughing?
Is the baby one today?
Is the teenager giving the baby a present?
Is the baby happy?
What is the baby doing?
Who is giving the present?

Methodology note

Remember at this stage that you are working on **identification** of the two types of question from the intonation pattern as much as the form. Practise producing the two types as in Exercise B.

Language and culture note

Point out, if necessary, that the answer to *Is this* is *Yes, it is./No, it isn't.*, not *Yes, this is.*, etc.

Exercise C

Repeat the procedure for Exercise B.

Tapescript

Presenter: **C 1 Listen and find.**
Voice: These people are getting married. The man is on the left and the woman is on the right. The man's family is behind him. The woman's family is behind her. There are more guests at the back. The man is giving a ring to the woman. He is putting it on her finger.

Presenter:	C 2 Listen. Say *Yes* or *No*.
Voice:	Are the man and the woman married at the moment?
	Are they single?
	Are they getting married?
	Will they be married in a few minutes?

Presenter:	C 3 Listen. Give information.
Voice:	How many people are in the picture?
	How many children?
	Where is the man's family?
	Where is the woman's family?
	What is the man doing?

Presenter:	C 4 Listen. Say *Yes*, *No*, or give information.
Voice:	How many people are in the picture?
	What is the man at the front doing?
	Where is the man's family?
	Are the man and the woman single at the moment?
	Are they getting married?
	How many children are in the picture?
	Where is the woman's family?
	Is the woman putting a ring on the man's finger?

	Andrew was born over 40 years ago.	True
	He died three years ago.	It depends when you do the lesson!

2	Is Andrew Jones dead?	Yes, he is.
	When did he die?	In 2004.
	Was he born in 1942?	No, he wasn't.
	When was he born?	In 1962.
	Was he twenty-four years old?	No, he wasn't.
	How old was he?	He was 42.

Tapescript

Presenter:	D 1 Listen. True or false?
Voice:	Andrew Jones is dead.
	He was born in 1942.
	He died in 2003.
	He was forty-one years old.
	Andrew was born over forty years ago.
	He died three years ago.

Presenter:	D 2 Listen. Say *Yes*, *No*, or give information.
Voice:	Is Andrew Jones dead?
	When did he die?
	Was he born in 1942?
	When was he born?
	Was he twenty-four years old?
	How old was he?

Exercise D

1 On this occasion, just get students to say *True* or *False*, plus the correction. The correction does not have to be in a full sentence with perfect structure.
2 Follow the procedure for mixed questions.

Answers

1	Andrew Jones is dead.	True
	He was born in 1942.	False – 1962
	He died in 2003.	False – 2004
	He was 41 years old.	False – 42

Exercise E

Give students time to read the questions. Elicit some ideas about customs in the UK – students may be very familiar with them and may even be able to explain in good English. However, do not confirm or correct at this stage.

Set for individual work and pairwork checking. Play the tape. Pause after each life event, if necessary, for students to make a note. Give time for checking, then feed back.

Answers

Possible answers:

has a birthday = presents
gets married = ring
dies = stone

Tapescript

Presenter: **E Listen to a short lecture about customs in the UK.**

Voice: Everybody is born, aren't they? Everybody dies, don't they? Most people get married. These three life events, birth, marriage and death, are important in most cultures. In the UK, we do special things on birthdays, when people get married and when a person dies.

When a person has a birthday, friends and family give the person presents. A present for a child is often a toy, but people sometimes give money.

When people get married, the man puts a ring on the woman's finger. He puts it on the third finger of her left hand. Sometimes the woman puts a ring on the man's finger.

When a person dies, the family often buys a stone. On the stone, they put the name of the person, the date of his or her birth and the date of his or her death. They sometimes put a sentence about the person.

Exercise F

Elicit a few ideas, then put students in pairs to discuss. Allow plenty of time for discussion if you can make pairs of students from different cultures. Feed back.

Closure

Ask students mixed questions about the pictures. See if they can identify perfectly the two types of question.

Lesson 2: Listening

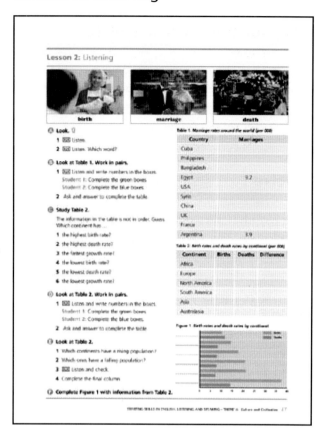

Introduction

Say the stressed syllable of the key multi-syllable words from Lesson 1. Students identify the full word.

fam	family
marr	married
par	party
pres /z/	present (n)
sing	single
ad	adult
ba	baby
chil /aɪ/	children
fe /iː/	female
peo /iː/	people
per /ɜː/	person
teen	teenager
wo /ʊ/	woman
wo /ɪ/	women

Exercise A

1   Refer students to the three pictures. Give students time to look at the pictures and each word. Play the three words.
2   Point out that students must be able to pick out words from the stream of speech. Play each sentence and get students to point to the correct picture and/or say the word.

Tapescript

Presenter:	Lesson 2
	A 1 Listen.
Voice:	birth
	marriage
	death

Presenter:	A 2 Listen. Which word?
Voice:	Some countries have a very high birth rate.
	The marriage rate in Cuba is very high.
	Do you know the death rate in your country?
	We talk about birth rate per thousand people in a country.
	The death rate in Africa is thirty-seven per thousand people.
	Countries in Western Europe have a low marriage rate.

Methodology note

It is vital that you give students practice in hearing new words in the stream of speech. A word such as *birth* will sound quite different if followed by, e.g., *rate*, when the sound will be something like *bir thrate*.

Exercise B

Refer students to Table 1.

1   Give students time to look at the table and work out what it shows. Then ask some quick checking questions. Make sure students have some idea where each country in the list is in the world, i.e., the continent (see the Closure). Make sure they can also interpret the idea of *per 000*, e.g., the figure for the marriage rate in Egypt is 9.2, which means there are 9.2 marriages per 1000 people each year, or .92 per hundred, nearly 1%. Elicit the idea that the table is probably in numerical order – because it is not in alphabetical – so Cuba will be the biggest number, and Argentina the lowest, with the others in between.

2   Set for pairwork. Make sure students understand that they are only listening for half of the information. Play the tape. Put students in pairs to exchange information. Monitor and assist. Feed back, building up the table on the board.

Answers

Country	Marriages
Cuba	17.7
Philippines	14.0
Bangladesh	10.7
Egypt	9.2
USA	8.9
Syria	8.6
China	7.7
UK	5.9
France	4.4
Argentina	3.9

Tapescript

Presenter: B 1 Listen and write numbers in the boxes.

Voice: Marriage is very popular in most countries of the world, but there are big differences in marriage rates. Cuba and the Philippines have high rates, for example. Cuba has one of the highest rates at seventeen point seven per thousand people, while the Philippines is close behind with fourteen. Many countries in Western Europe have low rates, for example the UK and France. The UK has five point nine, while France has one of the lowest rates at four point four. However, the lowest rate of all is Argentina, at three point nine. Many countries have a rate around ten. Bangladesh has ten point seven, Egypt has nine point two, the USA has eight point nine and Syria is slightly lower at eight point six. China has a rate of seven point seven.

Exercise C

Refer students to Table 2. Repeat checking questions, but ask students to ignore the final column of the table for the moment. Elicit ideas, but do not confirm or correct.

Language and culture note

Students may be quite good at guessing, particularly for their own continent. For example, they may mention Aids and famine or starvation, etc., as a cause of lots of deaths in Africa, and perhaps small families in Europe as a cause of low birth rate in that continent.

Exercise D

1 Repeat the procedure for Exercise B. Play the tape.
2 Put students in pairs to exchange information. Monitor and assist. Feed back, building up the table on the board.

Answers
After Exercise E.

Tapescript

Presenter: **D 1 Listen and write numbers in the boxes.**

Voice: There are big differences between birth rate and death rate in different continents. Africa has the highest birth rate at thirty-seven births per thousand people, but it also has the highest death rate – fourteen per thousand. Europe has the lowest birth rate at ten point five per thousand, but quite a high death rate, too, at twelve. Why does Europe have a high death rate? Because Europe has an old population – nearly twenty percent of people in Europe are over sixty-five years of age. There are big differences in the birth rate in the Americas. In North America, the birth rate is fourteen, but in South America it is twenty-one point five. The death rates are very similar. North America has a death rate of eight point five and South America seven point five. The birth rate in Asia is similar to South America. It is twenty-one. In Australasia it is lower, at eighteen, but Asia and Australasia have the same death rate – eight.

Exercise E

Establish the importance of the final column of Table 2. Point out that the difference between births and deaths will be the growth rate. So if twenty people in a thousand are born each year and ten die, there will be a growth rate of ten per thousand, or one per hundred, i.e., 1%.

1, 2 Set for pairwork. Do not feed back.
3 Play the tape.
4 Put students back into pairs to complete the final column. Feed back, adding the information to the column and eliciting the interpretation.

Answers

Continent	Births	Deaths	Difference	Interpretation	Questions in Exercise C
Africa	37.0	14.0	23.0	*growing very fast*	*the highest birth rate, the highest death rate and the fastest growth rate*
Europe	10.5	12.0	-1.5	*falling slightly*	*the lowest birth rate and the lowest growth rate*
North America	14.0	8.5	5.5	*growing slowly*	
South America	21.5	7.5	14.0	*growing fast*	*the lowest death rate*
Asia	21.0	8.0	13.0	*growing fast*	
Australasia	18.0	8.0	10.0	*growing quite fast*	

Tapescript

Presenter: E 3 Listen and check.

Voice: The population of the world is growing because the birth rate is higher than the death rate. Overall, the world birth rate is twenty-two and the death rate is nine. So the difference is twenty-two minus nine, which is thirteen per thousand people, or one point three percent. But there are big differences between the growth rates in different continents. Africa, for example, has a difference between birth rate and the death rate of twenty-three, whereas Europe has a difference of minus one point five. In other words, the population of Europe isn't rising. It's going down.

Exercise F

Refer students to the bar chart and elicit the meanings of the two bars in each case.

Put students in pairs to work out which bars depict the information for each continent.

Answers

Figure 1: *Birth rates and death rates by continent*

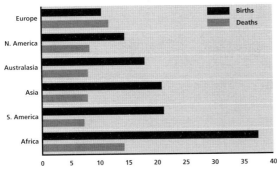

Closure

Say the names of countries and continents from this lesson at random. See if students can find the word on the page immediately. Say the names in isolation, then in a sentence from the tapescript.

You could even give students a test on the location of each country, i.e., you say a country and the students have to say the correct continent.

Answers

Country	Continent
Egypt	*Africa*
UK France	*Europe*
Cuba USA	*North America*
Argentina	*South America*
Syria China Bangladesh	*Asia*
Philippines	*Australasia*

Lesson 3: Speaking

Lesson 3: Speaking

diphthongs

1	2
die	age
child	baby
	male

Follow this procedure in each case.

1 Say a word from each pair several times, e.g., *party – family*. Do not let students say anything.
2 Isolate the vowel sounds. Do not let students say anything.
3 Say each pair of stressed vowels for students to repeat chorally.
4 Say each pair of vowels for individual students to repeat.
5 Write the pair of words on the board, in a column marked *1* or *2* (see the tables).
6 Say the vowel sound of one of the two words from the pair. Students must say *1* or *2*.
7 As you do more and more pairs, go back over the previous pairs until you are saying sounds from random from the whole set.

Introduction

Revise the main vowel sounds with words connected with culture and civilization.

long vs short
(based on the stressed syllable in each case)

1	2
party	family
	thank
	married
	marriage
female	single
people	children
teenage	
born	old (dark *l*)
group	young
girl	dead
person	death
birth	present
	guest
	friend

Put students into pairs to do the minimal pairs activity below. Each student says one word from each pair and the other tries to work out which. Point out that these are all English words, although the meanings are not important.

1	2
heart	hat
hurt	het
heat	hit
haughty	hotty
how	hoe
hate	height

Exercise A

Give students plenty of time to study the pictures and work out what is going on.

1 Set for pairwork. Feed back.
2 Set for pairwork. Feed back.
3 Encourage students to make full sentences or descriptions. Elicit from individuals.
4 Set for pairwork. Monitor and assist. Allow the partner to help the student trying to remember a picture.

Answers

1 A a child's birthday party
  B death – students may want to say *putting the body in the ground / funeral / burial*, or similar, which is fine.
  C a family celebration/dinner (e.g., Thanksgiving)
  D marriage
  E birth
  F a family party (e.g., New Year's Eve)
2 One logical order is E, A, D, C/F, B, but there are others.
3 Depend on the students.
4 Depend on the students.

Language and culture note

We normally describe photographs in English as if the events are happening now. Remind students of the use of the present continuous for this, e.g., *two people are getting married*. This is good contrast with the use of the present continuous to describe trends, which was exemplified in the first two lessons of this theme, and will be picked up on later.

Exercise B

Make sure students are ready, as you can only usefully play the sounds once. Ask students to put up their hands when they can name the life event, but not to speak. Ideally, all or most hands should shoot up at the first strains. Invite students to name the event. Do not accept the letter of the picture as an answer.

Answers

1 E birth
2 D marriage
3 C a dinner party
4 B death
5 A a birthday party

Tapescript

    Presenter: Lesson 3
              B Listen. Which picture?
  Sound effects: 1 birth – a baby's first cries
              2 marriage – organ music, church bells
              3 dinner party – plates clacking together and hum of conversation
              4 death – a passing bell
              5 birthday party – general hubbub and children's music

Methodology note

We need to give students as many possible associations between the real world and the sight and sound of a word. The more associations, the more quickly the brain should be able to retrieve the word when it is needed.

Exercise C

Refer students to the rebus pictures.

1 Play the tape.
2 Play the tape again, pausing after each question and inviting students to answer before playing the answer. Deal with any pronunciation problems.
3 Elicit the first question, then play the tape again, pausing after each answer this time and eliciting the next question. Deal with intonation of different types of questions.

Work through the points in the Skills Check.

Tapescript

Presenter: C 1 Listen.

Voice 1:   When were you born?

Voice 2:   In 1976.

Voice 1:   So you are 29?

Voice 2:   No, I'm not. I'm 30.

Voice 1:   Are you married?

Voice 2:   Yes, I am.

Voice 1:   When did you get married?

Voice 2:   Oh, in 1997.

Voice 1:   Have you got any children?

Voice 2:   Yes, I have. Three. Two boys and a girl.

Voice 1:   What does your father do?

Voice 2:   He's dead, actually.

Voice 1:   Oh, I'm sorry.

Voice 2:   Thank you.

Voice 1:   When did he die?

Voice 2:   In 2004.

Presenter: C 2 Listen and answer.
[REPEAT OF EXERCISE C1]

Presenter: C 3 Listen and ask.
[REPEAT OF EXERCISE C1]

Exercise D

1 Set for pairwork. Make sure students realize that they have to give true information this time.
2 Elicit information from individuals about their partner.

Closure

1 Ask mixed questions about life events and get individual students to reply.
2 Invite students to ask you about your life events. Answer truthfully, if possible.

Lesson 4: Speaking

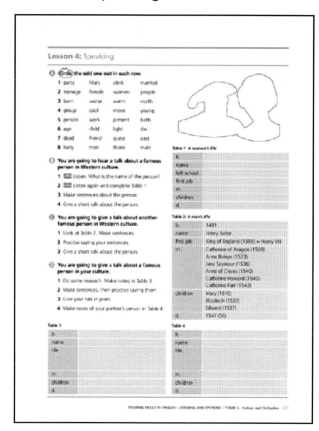

Introduction

Play *The Alphabet Game* with words connected with families, culture and civilization. Ask students to try to think of at least one word beginning with each letter of the alphabet. Give clues, including mime and drawings.

Answers

Possible answers:

A *adult, age, aunt*
B *baby, birth, born, boy*
C *child, children, civilization, culture, custom*
D *(daughter), dead, die*
E *Easter* (Christian festival), *Eid* (Arabic festival)
F *family, father, female, friend*
G *girl, group, guest*
H *home, house, (husband)*
I *(in-laws)*
J ?
K ?

L ?
M *man, married, men, mother*
N ?
O *old*
P *party, people, person, present*
Q ?
R *rate* (as in *birth rate*, etc.), *ring*
S *single, stone* (as in *headstone*)
T *teenager, thank*
U *(uncle)*
V ?
W *(wife), woman, women*
X ?
Y *young*
Z ?

Note that the words in brackets have not been formally presented, but students may know them.

Exercise A

Set for individual work and pairwork checking. If students are struggling, work through the words in the first row, exaggerating the stressed vowel. Feed back orally.

Answers

1	party	Mars	clerk	*married*	/æ/, not /ɑː/
2	teenage	female	*women*	people	/ɪ/, not /iː/
3	born	*worse*	warm	north	/ɜː/, not /ɔː/
4	group	cool*	move	*young*	/ʌ/, not /uː/
5	person	work	*present*	birth	/e/, not /ɜː/
6	*age*	child	light	die	/eɪ/, not /aɪ/
7	dead	friend	guest	*east*	/iː/, not /e/
8	baby	train	*thank*	male	/æ/, not /eɪ/

*The dark *l* changes the vowel quality, but it starts as /uː/.

Exercise B

1 Set for individual work and pairwork checking. Play the tape. Feed back orally.
2 Set for individual work and pairwork checking. Play the tape. Feed back, building up model notes on the board.
3 Elicit sentences from individual students. Correct for pronunciation and structure.
4 Allow students time to compose a short talk. Monitor and assist. Get students to give their talks in pairs and correct each other.

Answers

1 Princess Diana
2 Model notes:

b.	1961
name	Spencer
left school	16
first job	1979 – pre-school
m.	1981 – Charles Windsor
children	William (1982)
	Harry (1984)
d.	1997 (36)

Tapescript

Presenter: Lesson 4
B 1 **Listen. What is the name of the person?**

Voice: She was born in 1961. Her family name was Spencer. She was not very good at school. She left when she was sixteen. In 1979, she started work in a pre-school. In 1981, she got married. Her husband was called Charles Windsor. She had two sons. William was born in 1982, and Harry was born in 1984. Her marriage was not a good one. She and Charles separated in 1992. She started doing a lot of work for poor people. On 31st August, 1997, she died in a car accident in Paris. She was thirty-six years old.

Tapescript

Presenter: B 2 **Listen again and complete Table 1.**
[REPEAT OF EXERCISE B1]

Exercise C

If students do not know about Henry VIII, tell them briefly about him.
1 Set for pairwork. Monitor and assist.
2 Elicit sentences from individuals. Correct pronunciation and structure.
3 Allow students time to compose a short talk. Monitor and assist. Get students to give their talks in pairs and correct each other.

Language and culture note

If students are going to study wholly or partly in English, it is likely that they will come across references to iconic figures from Western, and particularly British and American, culture. They will need to use real-world knowledge to make sense of these references.

Exercise D

Follow the detailed instructions. Monitor and assist during the talks.

Closure

Make sure students understand and can produce all the key words from this theme, with good pronunciation and stress.

THEME 7 They Made Our World

General note

By the end of this theme, students should be able to hear and identify, in isolation and in context, the following words linked with transport. They should also be able to say them with reasonable pronunciation, especially stress in multi-syllable words, and use them in simple S V (O) (C) sentences and compound S V (O) (C) *when* S V (O) (C) sentences.

accident	driver	pedestrian	sailor
airport	land	pilot	street
arrive	leave	port	take off
bus station	passenger	railway station	traffic

In the listening activities in Lesson 1, there are two structure points which have not been formally dealt with to date:

1 Present perfect for events in the past with a present effect or consequence, e.g., *There has been an accident./ Have you ever had an accident?*

2 *was doing when did* and *did when did*

These are for comprehension only at this stage. They are analysed and practised later.

Lesson 1: Listening

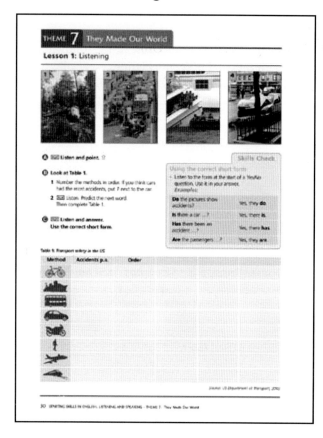

Introduction

Students may already be familiar with the following words from this lexical set:

bicycle	drive	road
boat	fly	sail
bus	go	ship
car	motorbike	train
come	plane	walk

If you are in any doubt, check that all the students can identify and produce these words in isolation.

1 Check or teach the related words, e.g., *plane – fly*, etc.
2 Mime forms of transport. Get students to mime them when you say or flash the word.
3 Ask students to put the forms of transport into order of speed – slowest first.

Then put some, or all, of the words into sentence context.

Exercise A

Give students plenty of time to look at all four pictures before starting the tape.

Play the tape. The first items are revision.

Tapescript

Presenter:	Theme 7 They Made Our World
	Lesson 1
	A Listen and point.
Voice:	ship
	cars
	plane
	road
	trees
	sea
	people
	sailors
	sky
	traffic
	driver
	accident
	crash
	passengers
	pedestrians
	street

Voice:	A car hit another car.
	The accident has caused a traffic jam.
	There are men in the road.
	The passengers are getting off the ship.
	The plane has crashed.
	The ship hit another ship.
	The ship is going down.
	There's a plane in the forest.
	Two people are crossing the road.
	There has been an accident on the main road.
	They're going to take the cars away.
	The ship is going to go under the water.
	The taxi has had a crash.

Methodology note

These pictures, and some others in this theme, are quite shocking. The writer believes this is acceptable in a language classroom since it should not be an emotional desert. However, be prepared for students to be shocked by the pictures. Deal with the issue sensitively.

Language and culture note

Make sure students realize that a *pedestrian* is not just someone walking, but someone walking near traffic. So being a pedestrian is a dangerous thing, whereas walking per se is not.

Exercise B

Check or teach the word *measure*. Ask students *How can we measure time / length / temperature?*

1 Refer students to Table 1. Check or teach the word *transport*. Elicit the methods of transport from the first column.
2 Remind students that they should always predict content before they listen. This will help them to understand when they hear something, even if their prediction is wrong. Set for individual work and pairwork checking. Play up to the first pause and elicit ideas. Then play the true information. Reassure students that it does not matter if they were wrong – the important thing is that they know what the speaker is going to talk about. Then play up to the first number and check that students are filling the table correctly. Continue with the rest of the items.

Feed back, ideally onto a datashow or OHT. Get students to work out the order and compare that with their own prediction.

Answers

Method	Accidents p.a.	Order
bicycle	58,000	3
boat/ship	8,000	6
bus	17,000	5
car	2,378,000	1
motorbike	54,000	4
pedestrians	77,000	2
plane	1,700	8
train	3,000	7

Tapescript

Presenter: B 2 **Listen. Predict the next word. Then complete Table 1.**

Voice: What is the safest method of transport? Actually, we can't answer that question before we answer another one. How can we **measure** safety? One way is to look at the number of accidents for each method. In America in 2002, the largest number of accidents involved [PAUSE] cars. There were two million, three hundred and seventy-eight thousand car accidents. In second place was accidents involving [PAUSE] pedestrians, that is, people walking near roads or crossing roads. There were seventy-seven thousand accidents involving pedestrians. In third place, we have accidents involving [PAUSE] bicycles. There were fifty-eight thousand accidents with cyclists. That is slightly more than accidents involving [PAUSE] motorbikes – the figure there was fifty-four thousand. Buses were much safer in this way of measuring. There were only seventeen thousand bus accidents, but that is still more than twice the number of [PAUSE] boat or ship accidents – eight thousand. Finally, we have very small numbers for [PAUSE] trains and planes – three thousand accidents involving trains, and one thousand, seven hundred involving planes.

Exercise C

Refer students to the Skills Check. Drill the examples. Elicit the negative short answer in each case.

Set for choral response, but make sure that students do not call out until you have given everyone a chance to think of the correct response. Play the tape, pausing after each question. Replay the question if a significant number of students get any one wrong.

Tapescript

Presenter: C Listen and answer.
Use the correct short form.

Voice: Do all the pictures show accidents?
Does the first picture show a plane crash?
Is there a motorcycle in the fourth picture?
Has there been a road accident in the second picture?
Are the passengers getting off the ship in the third picture?
Is there a traffic jam in the second picture?
Are there passengers in the first picture?
Are the men crossing the road in the fourth picture policemen?
Were all the cars in the second picture involved in the accident?
Did the ship in the third picture hit a small boat?
Was the taxi in the fourth picture involved in an accident?

Methodology notes

1 Note that a lot of these sentences are deliberately long, so that students have had time to forget the grammatical form by the time they come to answer.
2 Note that in English, students have to also work out the correct preposition to use. You might want to drill some of the expressions and the related prepositions, e.g., *Are the people ...?/ Yes, they are.* Then do the set of questions again, for individual students to respond to.
3 If anyone asks about the present perfect questions, e.g., *Has there been an accident ...?*, point out that we often use this form in British English to ask a general question. Say it will be explained further later.

Language and culture notes

1 Many languages have an all-purpose *Yes, it's true* type of response to these *Yes/No* questions. In other words, they may not expect to have to pay attention to the grammar of the question when forming their answer. You might like to ask students about this point in their own language(s).
2 For some reason, we do not seem to collocate *plane* or *train* with *accident*. We normally say *plane/train crash*.

Closure

Ask students *Have you ever had an accident?* When you get a positive answer from a student, ask more questions with the past simple, e.g., *How old were you? Where were you? Were you in a car?* If you have a group of teenagers, ask them silly questions like *Were you driving?*, etc. Avoid *What happened?*, as this would be difficult for a student at this level to answer, particularly until you have looked at the past continuous later in this theme.

Lesson 2: Listening

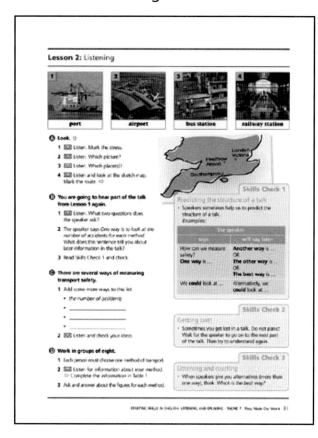

Introduction

Say the stressed syllable of the key multi-syllable words from Lesson 1. Students identify the full word.

bi	'bicycle
dri	'driver
mo	'motorbike/'motorcyclist
des	pe'destrian
tra	'traffic
ac	'accident
sai	'sailor
pa	'passengers

Methodology note

As noted before, this is still recognition. Do not worry about pronunciation of target words, as long as they are recognizable.

Exercise A

1   Refer students to the four pictures. Give students time to look at the pictures and each word. Play the four words.
2   Point out that students must be able to pick out words from the stream of speech. Play each sentence and get students to point to the correct picture and/or say the word.
3   Point out that some words go with one kind of transport, e.g., *take off* = *plane*. Other words can go with several forms of transport, e.g., *arrive*. Ask students to list and say the letter(s) of the correct form(s) of transport in each case.
4   Refer students to the sketch map. Tell them to listen and follow the route.

Tapescript

Presenter:	Lesson 2
	A 1 Listen. Mark the stress.
Voice:	port
	airport
	bus station
	railway station

Presenter:	**A 2 Listen. Which picture?**
Voice:	How far is the airport from here?
	Is there a railway station near here?
	Can you tell me the way to the bus station?
	Is there a port in this city?

Presenter:	**A 3 Listen. Which place(s)?**
Voice:	land
	take off
	arrive
	leave
	fly
	sail
	go
	come

Presenter: **A 4 Listen and look at the sketch map. Mark the route.**

Voice: When the ship gets to the port in Southampton, you must go to the railway station and get a train to London Victoria. Find the bus station – it's very close to the railway station – and from there, you can get a bus to the airport – it's called Heathrow.

Exercise B

1 Set for individual work and pairwork checking. Play the tape. Feed back, getting the two questions on the board.
2 Write the key sentence on the board: *One way is to look at the number of accidents for each method.* Underline *One way*, if students are struggling, but do not confirm or correct. Refer them to Skills Check 1.
3 Give students time to read the Skills Check. Then work through the points carefully.

Answers
1 What is the safest method of transport?
   How can we measure safety?
2, 3 See Skills Check 1.

Tapescript
Presenter: **B 1 Listen. What two questions does the speaker ask?**

Voice: What is the safest method of transport? Actually, we can't answer that question before we answer another one. How can we measure safety? One way is to look at the number of accidents for each method.

Exercise C

Set for individual work and pairwork checking. Play the tape. Feed back, building up the list on the board. Check or teach the ideas contained in the list, especially the chance of doing something. Point out that you have a chance of dying from lightning at some time in your life of 1 in 56,000.

Get students to add these methods to the next three columns of Table 1 on page 31.

Answers
* the number of accidents
* the number of deaths
* the number of deaths per passenger km
* the chances of dying

Table 1: *Transport safety in the US*

Method	Accidents p.a.	Order	Deaths p.a.	Deaths per passenger km	Chance: 1 in …
bicycle					

Tapescript
Presenter: **C 2 Listen and check your ideas.**

Voice: How can we measure transport safety? One way is to look at the number of accidents for each method. Another way is to look at the number of deaths by each method. Do more people die each year in car accidents or plane crashes, for example? We could look at the distance that people travel by each method each year. For example, people travel much further by car than by bicycle, so we could measure the deaths per passenger kilometre. Finally, we could consider the chance of having a fatal accident – an accident in which someone dies – by each method. There aren't many plane crashes every year, but when a plane crashes, most passengers die. On the other hand, there are millions of car accidents every year, but in most cases, nobody dies.

Exercise D

Make sure students understand the task. Elicit from a number of students which method they are going to listen for. Play the tape. Feed back, ideally onto a datashow or an OHT.

Answers

Table 1: *Transport safety in the US*

Method	Accidents p.a.	Deaths p.a.	Deaths per billion passenger km	Chance: 1 in ...
pedestrians	77,000	5,307	49	612
car	2,378,000	40,000	2.8	869
motorbike	54,000	2,106	112	1,159
bicycle	58,000	813	41	4,857
boat/ship	8,000	819	0.04	9,019
plane	1,700	635	0.02	20,015
bus	17,000	17	0.06	86,628
train	3,000	1,096	0.9	133,035

Tapescript

Presenter: D 2 **Listen for information about your method. Complete the information in Table 1.**

Voice: As we have seen, there are four main ways to measure transport safety. We have looked at accidents. What about the figures for the other ways? Firstly, let's look at deaths per year. Once again, cars are the most dangerous method of travel. There were forty thousand deaths in 2002 in car accidents. In second place were pedestrians. There were five thousand, three hundred and seven deaths of pedestrians. Motorcyclists were in third place, but a long way behind. Two thousand, one hundred and six people died in accidents involving motorcyclists. Less than half that number died in train accidents. The actual figure was one thousand and ninety-six. Cyclists and ship passengers had very similar results – eight hundred and thirteen people died in cycling accidents, and eight hundred and nineteen in boating or shipping accidents. Plane passengers were a little way behind at six hundred and thirty-five. Finally, what about bus passengers? Only seventeen people died on buses in the US in 2002.

Another way to measure transport safety is to look at deaths per kilometre. Actually, this is impossible because the figure would be so small. So we measure deaths per billion passenger kilometres. A billion is a number followed by nine zeros. We have a new number one if we measure transport safety in this way. It is motorcyclists. There were one hundred and twelve deaths per billion passenger kilometres by motorcyclists in the US in 2002. Pedestrians were in second place, forty-nine deaths, with cyclists third at forty-one deaths. Car accidents are in fourth place by this measure. Only two point eight deaths per billion passenger kilometres. Trains caused nought point nine, and then we have some very small numbers – ships point nought four, buses point nought six, and planes point nought two.

Finally, what is the actual chance of dying during your lifetime in a particular kind of transport accident? Of course in this case, a low figure is bad. I mean, if you have a one in two chance, that is very, very bad, but a one in two thousand chance is much better. So how do the different transport methods do by this measure? It seems you have the biggest chance of dying as a pedestrian – one in six hundred and twelve. Next, we have car accidents – one in eight hundred and sixty-nine. Motorbikes are in third place – one in one thousand, one hundred and fifty-nine. Then the figure jumps to cyclists, four thousand, eight hundred and fifty-seven, and then doubles to ship accidents, one in nine thousand and nineteen. It doubles again to plane accidents to one in twenty thousand and fifteen, and then leaps for bus accidents to one in eighty-six thousand, six hundred and twenty-eight. The safest way to travel, according to this measure, is the train. The chance of dying in a train accident is just one in one hundred and thirty-three thousand and thirty-five. Compare this with the chance of being hit by lightning – one in fifty-six thousand – and you will see how small the chance is.

Methodology note

As Skills Check 2 states, students will always get lost at some time during a talk. They need to have predicted the structure of the talk so they have a way back into the talk. In this case, they can predict that the speaker will talk about the methods in order, so if they get lost in one set of figures, they can wait until the speaker starts to talk about another set. The activity in Exercise D is an extreme version of waiting. In this case, they have to wait until their method of transport is mentioned each time, and take no notice of any of the other information.

Closure

Ask a large number of questions about the information in each column of the table with comparatives. Make sure you use some with *safe*, and some with *dangerous*, so students get exposure to the two forms of comparative, i.e., *-er/more than*. For example, *Look at the column of accidents. Are cars safer than motorbikes? Are planes more dangerous than trains?*, etc. Put students into pairs to ask similar questions. Then ask *For each method, what is the safest/most dangerous method of transport?*

Ask *Which is the best way to measure transport safety?* Ask students to look at all the figures and decide. Get them to write their final order in the last column. Feed back and discuss findings.

Answers
Clearly there is no right answer to the final question, but it does seem that planes, buses and trains are very safe compared with cars, bicycles, motorbikes and walking near roads.

Lesson 3: Speaking

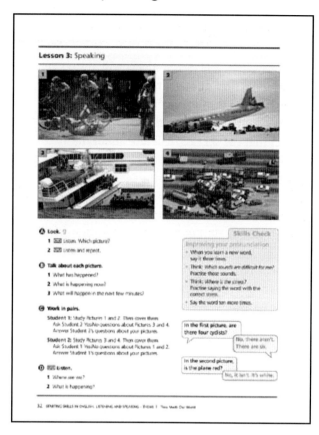

Introduction

Revise the main vowel sounds with words connected with technology and positions in a table.

long vs short
(based on the stressed syllable in each case)

1	2
car last (place)	passenger accident traffic land crash
leave street	ship fifth (place)
port walk fourth (place)	(get) off
group bus	come
first/third (place)	pedestrian

diphthongs

1	2
fly drive bicycle pilot arrive	plane train sail railway station take (off)
motorbike boat go road	(go) down

Follow this procedure in each case.

1 Say a word from each pair several times, e.g., *car – accident*. Do not let students say anything.
2 Isolate the vowel sounds. Do not let students say anything.
3 Say each pair of stressed vowels for students to repeat chorally.
4 Say each pair of vowels for individual students to repeat.
5 Write the pair of words on the board, in a column marked *1* or *2* (see the tables).
6 Say the vowel sound of one of the two words from the pair. Students must say *1* or *2*.
7 As you do more and more pairs, go back over the previous pairs until you are saying sounds from random from the whole set.

Put students into pairs to do the minimal pairs* activity below. Each student says one word from each pair and the other tries to work out which. Point out that these are all English words, although the meanings are not important.

1	2
barter	bad
Bert	bed
beat	bid
bought	bod
about	abode
abate	abide

*These are not really minimal pairs, but the differences are slight.

Exercise A

1   Give students plenty of time to look at the four pictures. Set for individual work and pairwork checking. Play the short texts, pausing after each one for students to choose and check with their partner, but do not let them shout out. At the end of the four extracts, ask students *What's happened in picture 1 / 2 / 3 / 4?* Try to elicit the *has done* form.

2   Play the tape or say the individual sentences. Students repeat.

Deal with tense selection here. We use *has done* (present perfect) because the action happened in the past, but we can still see the result – the bicycles on the ground, the plane on the snow, the smoke and the wreckage.

Answers

Picture 3
Picture 1
Picture 2
Picture 4

Tapescript

Presenter: Lesson 3
            A 1 Listen. Which picture?
Voice: A fire has started on the ship. The passengers are getting off the ship. The sailors are helping them.

            Two bikes have crashed in the road. Some other cyclists are riding past. They are in a race. There are people watching on the other side of the road.

            A plane has crashed in Antarctica. It is in the snow.

            There has been a terrible accident. Lots of cars are involved.

Presenter: A 2 Listen and repeat.
Voice: Two bikes have crashed in the road.
            A plane has crashed in Antarctica.
            A fire has started on the ship.
            There has been a terrible accident.

Methodology note

If students are struggling with repeating the sentences, use backchaining, i.e.,

You say: *the road*
Students say: *the road*
You say: *the side of the road*
Students say: *the side of the road*
You say: *crashed at the side of the road*, etc.

Exercise B

Work through picture 1 as an example, i.e.,
1   Two bikes have crashed in the road.
2   Other cyclists are riding past.
3   Perhaps some cyclists will stop to help.
Set for pairwork. Monitor and assist. Get some students to talk about a picture for the whole class.

Exercise C

Remind students about *Yes/No* questions. Give some related to the pictures, then elicit some more. Demonstrate the activity with a good student. Set for pairwork. Monitor and assist.

Exercise D

Tell students they are going to hear some sounds. They must work out where and what is happening. Set for pairwork. Play the tape, pausing after each sound for students to discuss, then elicit feedback.

Answers

1 airport
2 sea port
3 bus station
4 railway station
5 busy road
6 city street

Tapescript

Presenter: **D Listen.**

Sound effects:
1 airport sounds, with a plane taking off
2 a ship sounding its foghorn
3 a bus station – buses coming and going
4 announcements and the noise of trains at a railway station
5 a busy road, cars going by at high speed
6 a city street full of traffic

Closure

Work through the Skills Check, then put students into pairs to identify their own problem areas and follow the advice.

Lesson 4: Speaking

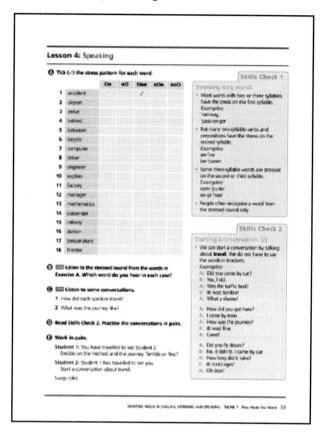

M *mile, motorbike*

N *near*

O ?

P *passenger, pedestrian, pilot, plane, port*

Q *(queue)*

R *railway station, road*

S *sail, sailor, sea, ship, sky, station, street*

T *take off, (taxi), traffic, train*

U ?

V *(van), (vehicle)*

W *walk, water, (wreck)*

X ?

Y ?

Z ?

Note that the words in brackets have not been formally presented, but students may know them.

Exercise A

Set for individual work and pairwork checking. Explain that some words have silent vowels – marked * in the Answers. Feed back. Work through Skills Check 1.

Answers

		Oo	oO	Ooo	oOo	ooO
1	accident			✓		
2	airport	✓				
3	arrive		✓			
4	behind		✓			
5	between		✓			
6	bicycle			✓		
7	computer				✓	
8	driver	✓				
9	engineer					✓
10	explain		✓			
11	factory*			✓		
12	manager			✓		
13	mathematics*				✓	
14	passenger			✓		
15	railway	✓				
16	station	✓				
17	temperature*				✓	
18	theatre				✓	

Introduction

Play *The Alphabet Game* with words connected with transport and accidents. Ask students to try to think of at least one word beginning with each letter of the alphabet. Give clues, including mime and drawings.

Answers
Possible answers:

A *accident, airport, arrive*

B *bicycle, boat, bus*

C *car, come, crash, cyclist*

D *deaths, (depart), drive, driver*

E *(engine)*

F *fly*

G *go*

H *hit, (hurt)*

I *(injured)*

J *jam, i.e, traffic jam*

K *kilometre*

L *leave, (lorry)*

Exercise B

Set for individual work and pairwork checking. Play each word and give students time to think, then elicit answers from individuals.

Answers

dri	*driver*
tween	*between*
ma	*mathematics*
ac	*accident*
sta	*station*
pass	*passenger*
plain	*explain*
rive	*arrive*
bi	*bicycle*
eat	*theatre*
man	*manager*
air	*airport*
pu	*computer*
fac	*factory*
rail	*railway*
temp	*temperature*
neer	*engineer*
hind	*behind*

Tapescript

Presenter: Lesson 4
B Listen to the stressed sound from the words in Exercise A. Which word do you hear in each case?

Voice: dri
tween
ma
ac
sta
pass
plain
rive
bi
eat
man
air
pu

fac
rail
temp
neer
hind

Exercise C

If you think students will realize that the conversations are printed in Skills Check 2, set the questions for pairwork discussion. Play each extract, then ask the two questions.

Tapescript

Presenter: C Listen to some conversations.
1
Voice 1: Did you come by car?
Voice 2: Yes, I did.
Voice 1: Was the traffic bad?
Voice 2: (It was) terrible!
Voice 1: What a shame!
2
Voice 1: How did you get here?
Voice 2: I came by train.
Voice 1: How was the journey?
Voice 2: (It was) fine.
Voice 1: Great!
3
Voice 1: Did you fly down?
Voice 2: No, (I didn't). I came by car.
Voice 1: How long did it take?
Voice 2: (It took) ages.
Voice 1: Oh dear!

Exercise D

Work through Skills Check 2. Drill the sentences, then the conversations.

Exercise E

Set for pairwork. Monitor and assist.

Closure

Tell students you have just arrived in the country/town. Get them to start a conversation with you. Remind them also about starting conversations by talking about the weather (Theme 4, Skills Check, page 21).

THEME 8 Art and Literature

General note

By the end of this theme, students should be able to hear and identify, in isolation and in context, the following words linked with genres of stories and films. They should also be able to say them with reasonable pronunciation, especially stress in multi-syllable words, and use them in simple S V (O) (C) sentences.

adventure	historical
cartoon	horror
comedy	love
crime	science fiction

They should also be able to identify, in isolation and in context, the following verbs, in the present and the past, simple and continuous.

bring	draw	run
build	feel	say
carry	find	speak
check	make	talk
climb	put	tell

In the listening activities in Lesson 1, there are reflexive pronouns, which have not been formally dealt with to date. They are for comprehension only at this stage. They are analyzed and practised later.

Lesson 1: Listening

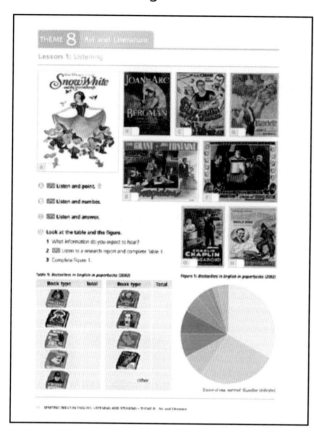

Introduction

Students may already be familiar with the following words from this lexical set:

architect	painter
architecture	painting
art	play
biographer	playwright
biography	poem
literature	poet
novel	sculptor
novelist	sculpture

They should also be very familiar with the following verbs, in the present and past, simple and continuous.

get	send
give	stop
meet	take
move	teach
paint	write
see	

If you are in any doubt, check that all the students can identify and produce these words in isolation.

1 Check or teach the related words, e.g., *architecture – architect*, etc.
2 Say words with an irregular past tense and ask students to say the irregular past, e.g., *get – got*.
3 Say irregular past tenses and ask students to say the infinitive.

Then put some or all of the words into sentence context.

Methodology note

Identifying the infinitive from the irregular past is a vital listening, and reading, skill. It is likely that we store words in a base form – in the case of English, it is the infinitive of a verb. Therefore, unless the brain can make a quick association between the irregular past, in speech and writing, and the infinitive, it will not be able to recover the meaning.

Exercise A

Give students plenty of time to look at all the pictures before saying or playing the tape. Play the tape.

Tapescript

Presenter:	Theme 8 Art and Literature
	Lesson 1
	A Listen and point.
Voice:	cartoon
	love story
	comedy
	science fiction
	crime
	historical
	horror
	adventure
Voice:	*Snow White* is a popular cartoon by Walt Disney.
	The French film industry makes a lot of love stories.

Alfred Hitchcock is famous for his crime films.

There are some very famous science fiction films.

Charlie Chaplin made a lot of comedy films in the 1920s.

Do you like historical films?

Mary Shelley wrote a book called *Frankenstein* in 1818. There are now many horror films about the monster in the book.

Daniel Defoe wrote a famous book called *The Adventures of Robinson Crusoe* in 1719. This novel is the basis of many films.

Language and culture notes

1 The word or phrase for a genre is sometimes an adjective, sometimes a noun, and sometimes a complete phrase, i.e.,

Adjective	Noun	Phrase
historical*	cartoon* comedy* crime* horror* adventure*	love story science fiction*

We can put most of these (marked with *) in front of the word *novel* or *film*. In the case of *love story*, there is a low-cover specific word – *romance*.

2 The pictures here show film posters, but the genres exist in novels, plays, TV programmes and films.

3 This theme is called Art and Literature. Is film art? Can it be literature? It is an interesting debate, but for current and future generations, it is likely that film and TV are more influential than novels (and painting), therefore worth dealing with in a language course.

Exercise B

Explain that students are going to hear a definition of each type of story. They should make a prediction about the type of story as soon as possible, but not shout out. Encourage them to write a number beside a picture in pencil, then change it if necessary as they get more information.

Answers

1	In this kind of film, the people often go on a journey. They must find something or someone. There are many dangers along the way. In some cases, they are in a difficult situation and they are in danger of dying.	*Adventure*
2	In this kind of story, there is a mystery. Someone is dead and the question is *Who did it?* There is a policeman, or a private detective, as the main person.	*Crime*
3	This kind of film makes you frightened. People do frightening things, or suddenly appear and make you jump.	*Horror*
4	This kind of film is set in the past. There are often kings or queens and famous events from history.	*Historical*
5	This kind of story has drawings. The drawings move. Nowadays, the drawings are often made by computer.	*Cartoon*
6	This kind of story is often very simple. One person loves another person, but for some reason, they cannot be together. The story is very simple, but very popular.	*Love story*
7	This kind of story is set in the future. There are often spaceships and people from other planets. Sometimes, people from the Earth go to another planet, sometimes people from another planet come to the Earth.	*Science fiction*
8	This kind of story makes you laugh. People do funny things or say funny things.	*Comedy*

Tapescript

Presenter: B **Listen and number.**

Voice: 1 In this kind of film, the people often go on a journey. They must find something or someone. There are many dangers along the way. In some cases, they are in a difficult situation and they are in danger of dying.

2 In this kind of story, there is a mystery. Someone is dead and the question is *Who did it?* There is a policeman, or a private detective, as the main person.

3 This kind of film makes you frightened. People do frightening things, or suddenly appear and make you jump.

4 This kind of film is set in the past. There are often kings or queens and famous events from history.

5 This kind of story has drawings. The drawings move. Nowadays, the drawings are often made by computer.

6 This kind of story is often very simple. One person loves another person, but for some reason, they cannot be together. The story is very simple, but very popular.

7 This kind of story is set in the future. There are often spaceships and people from other planets. Sometimes, people from the Earth go to another planet, sometimes people from another planet come to the Earth.

8 This kind of story makes you laugh. People do funny things or say funny things.

Exercise C

Remind students of the two kinds of questions. Say or play the first two as examples. Elicit answers. Point out or demonstrate the fall-rise at the end of *Yes/No*, and the high start of the information questions. Play the remaining questions, pausing after each question for students to think of an answer, then nominating one student to answer.

Answers

Questions with possible answers:

Do people often go on journeys in adventure stories?	*Yes, they do.*
What sort of person often appears in a crime story?	*A policeman or a detective.*
Are historical films set in the past?	*Yes, they are.*
What sort of people are historical films often about?	*Kings and queens.*
Are science fiction films often set in the future?	*Yes, they are.*
What happens in many science fiction films?	*People from the Earth go to another planet, or people from another planet come to the Earth.*
Do comedy films try to make you cry?	*No, they don't. They try to make you laugh.*
How do they do that?	*People do funny things or say funny things.*
Do horror films try to frighten you?	*Yes, they do.*
How do they do that?	*Things happen suddenly.*
Does a cartoon have real people in it?	*No, it doesn't.* * (See the Language and Culture note)
What does it have?	*Drawings, often animals.*

Tapescript

Presenter: C Listen and answer.

Voice: Do people often go on journeys in adventure stories?

What sort of person often appears in a crime story?

Are historical films set in the past?

What sort of people are historical films often about?

Are science fiction films often set in the future?

What happens in many science fiction films?

Do comedy films try to make you cry?

How do they do that?

Do horror films try to frighten you?

How do they do that?

Does a cartoon have real people in it?

What does it have?

Language and culture note

*Some students may point out that the appearance of real people in a cartoon is not unknown. Indeed, some of the first cartoon films by Walt Disney had both real people and drawings.

Methodology note

This time, students are exposed to mixed questions immediately. Make sure they are ready for this. Also note that you are looking for form as well as truth value at this stage of their learning. In other words, the answer to the first question is *Yes* = truth, *they do* = form. Both are important now.

Exercise D

Refer students to the table and the pie chart in Figure 1. Say that they should show the same information. Explain *bestseller* and *paperback* – ideally show one. Do not elicit names from the illustrations in the table – remember, this is largely a listening lesson.

1 Refer students to the pie chart. Ask what they expect to hear. They should be able to see that two parts occupy well over half of the area, with the other eight parts occupying the rest.

2 Set for individual work and pairwork checking. Play the tape, holding at each pause for students to suggest the next word, then complete the relevant entry in the table. Note that sometimes the next word is obvious, but sometimes you are simply looking for students to be thinking about possible content, even if their actual prediction is wrong. Feed back, building up the table on the board.

3 Set students in pairs to identify the colours for each type of book. They do not have to write anything, they can join the genre to the pie chart segment. Feed back, ideally onto an OHT of the pie chart. Clearly, the items which are the same size can be any of the correct answers.

Answers

Book type	Total
Adventure	1
Biography	1
Autobiography	4
Comedy	4
Crime	17
Historical	3
Horror	2
Love	14
Science fiction	4
other	2

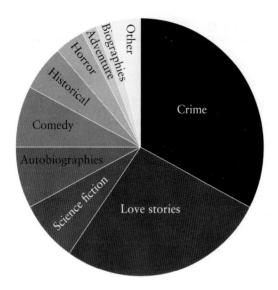

Source of raw material: Guardian Unlimited

Tapescript

Presenter: D 2 Listen to a research report and complete Table 1.

Voice: I am doing research into reading habits in English. I wanted to find out the most popular types of book in the English [PAUSE] language. I looked for information in libraries and on the [PAUSE] Internet. On the website of *The Guardian* newspaper, I found a list of best-selling paperback books for the year [PAUSE] 2002. I looked at the top fifty books in the list and I put them into separate categories – Crime, Adventure, [PAUSE] Horror, etc. Most of the categories are novels, but there are also [PAUSE] Biographies, or Life stories, and Autobiographies – Life stories written by people themselves. There is also the category Other, which means [PAUSE] true stories, cookery books, etc. If you look at Table 1, you will see my [PAUSE] results.

I found that two types of novel were far more [PAUSE] popular than the rest. In fact, these two types appear thirty-one times in *The Guardian* list of the first [PAUSE] fifty best-sellers. In other words, they account for over sixty [PAUSE] percent of the total. In first place, with seventeen out of fifty titles, that's thirty-four percent, is [PAUSE] Crime novels. Second, with only three fewer titles, we have [PAUSE] Love stories. In equal third place, with four titles each, are [PAUSE] Science fiction, Autobiography and Comedy novels. Just behind those three types we have [PAUSE] Historical novels with three titles, then [PAUSE] Horror and Other with two, and finally [PAUSE] Adventure and Biography with one each.

Closure

Ask students mixed questions about the table. See if they can identify perfectly the two types of question, and answer them with the correct information and correct forms.

Lesson 2: Listening

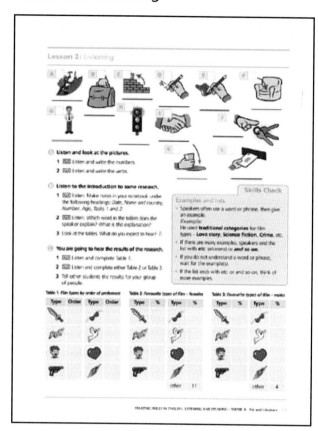

Introduction

Say the stressed syllable of the key multi-syllable words from Lesson 1. Students identify the full word.

toon	cartoon
com /kʌm/	comedy
sci /saɪ/	science
fic	fiction
horr	horror
sto /ɒ/	historical
ven	adventure
og	biography
au	autobiography
stor /stɔːr/	story

Methodology note

This is still recognition. Do not worry about pronunciation of target words, as long as they are recognizable.

Exercise A

1 Refer students to the illustrations. Give students time to look at them. Explain that they are going to hear the past tense of a verb in each case. They must write a number next to the correct picture.

2 Explain that this time they are going to hear the infinitive of each verb, which they must write.

Answers

1	C	1	built		2	sit
	B	2	carried			carry
	A	3	climbed			paint
	D	4	drew			stand
	J	5	found			draw
	I	6	met			send
	E	7	painted			find
	F	8	sat			climb
	G	9	stood			meet
	K	10	put			build
	H	11	stopped			put
	L	12	sent			stop

Tapescript

Presenter: Lesson 2
             A 1 Listen and write the numbers.
Voice: 1 built
          2 carried
          3 climbed
          4 drew
          5 found
          6 met
          7 painted
          8 sat
          9 stood
          10 put
          11 stopped
          12 sent

Presenter: **A 2 Listen and write the verbs.**

Voice: sit
carry
paint
stand
draw
send
find
climb
meet
build
put
stop

Methodology note

This is high-speed recognition of words which students should be very familiar with, although several have not been formally presented in this course. If you have any doubts about words, stop and work on them further. Clearly, students must be able to identify irregular verbs in speech, whether they hear the infinitive/present tense or the past simple form.

Exercise B

Refer students to the tables. Put them in pairs and say *What are you going to hear about?* Elicit some ideas, but do not confirm or correct.

1   Set for individual work and pairwork checking. Play the introduction. Feed back, building up the notes on the board.

2   Refer students to the tables again and ask *Which word is new in these tables?* Once again, do not confirm or correct. Set for individual work and pairwork checking. Play the second part of the talk. Feed back. Work through the Skills Check.

3   Set for pairwork. Feed back, but do not confirm or correct.

Answers

1

Date	1996
Name and country	Dr Stuart Fischoff USA
Number	560 (M = 264, F = 296)
Age	15–83
Tasks 1 and 2	put types of film in order (1 = fav.) name fav. film of all time

2   Possible answer:
Drama – a type of film; people have a problem and try to solve it.

3   Favourite types of films.

Tapescript

Presenter: **B 1 Listen. Make notes in your notebook under the following headings:** *Date, Name and country, Number, Age, Tasks 1 and 2.*

Introduction

Voice: I am going to talk about some research into types of films. In 1996, an American psychologist, Dr Stuart Fischoff, that's Stuart – S-T-U-A-R-T – Fischoff – F-I-S-C-H-O-F-F – did some research into films. He talked to five hundred and sixty people in the USA. There were two hundred and sixty-four men and two hundred and ninety-six women. They were between fifteen and eighty-three years old. He asked them to put different types of film in order – with 1 as their favourite. He also asked them to name their favourite film of all time. We can see some of the results of the research in the tables on the screen.

Presenter: B 2 Listen. Which word in the tables does the speaker explain? What is the explanation?

Voice: I must explain one word in these tables. The word is *Drama*. Dr Fischoff used traditional categories for film types, Love story, Science fiction, Crime, etc., but he also made a special category called Drama. A drama is usually a story at the theatre, but Dr Fischoff used this name for a particular type of film. In drama films, people have a problem. They try to solve the problem in various ways. Sometimes there is a crime in a drama story, but it is not the main point of the story. Sometimes love is part of a drama film, but it is not the main part. In most cases, the problem is with the people themselves. Perhaps they succeed. Perhaps they fail. Dramas teach us about life. Dr Fischoff found that a lot of popular films were dramas, not just crime stories, love stories, and so on.

Exercise C

1 Set for individual work and pairwork checking. Play the tape. Feed back, building up the table on the board.
2 Make sure students realize that they only have to listen for information for one of the tables. Play the tape. Do not feed back at this point.
3 Put students into pairs – one who has completed Table 2, and one who has completed Table 3. Monitor and assist. Feed back, building up the tables on the board.

Answers

Table 1: *Film types by order of preference*

Type	Order
Adventure	2
Cartoon	6
Comedy	5
Crime	8
Drama	1
Horror	7
Love	4
Science fiction	3

Table 2: *Favourite types of film – females*

Type	%
Adventure	15
Cartoon	4
Comedy	0
Crime	0
Drama	23
Horror	0
Love	31
Science fiction	16
other	11

Table 3: *Favourite types of film – males*

Type	%
Adventure	28
Cartoon	4
Comedy	0
Crime	0
Drama	32
Horror	0
Love	4
Science fiction	28
other	4

Methodology note

Clearly, if you have a mixed gender group, it is probably best to get the women to listen for Table 2 information and men to listen for Table 3.

Tapescript

Presenter: C 1 Listen and complete Table 1.

Voice: Dr Fischoff asked the first question of all five hundred and sixty people: *Can you put these types of film in order of preference, for example, if you like love stories the most, put 1.* The results are in Table 1. He found that drama films were the most popular type with the five hundred and sixty people. In second place were adventure films, followed by sci-fi, love and comedy films. In sixth place were cartoons, followed by horror films. Surprisingly, crime stories were in eighth and last place.

Presenter: C 2 Listen and complete either Table 2 or Table 3.

Voice: Dr Fischoff then asked the second question: *Can you name your favourite film of all time?* The results for women are in Table 2, and for men in Table 3. Not surprisingly, love stories came out on top. Thirty-one percent of women named love stories as their favourite type of film compared with only four percent of men. In second place for women was drama films, twenty-three percent chose this type, but drama films were top for men, thirty-two percent. Women put science fiction third, sixteen percent chose this type. This type of film was in equal second place for men, with twenty-eight percent. Adventure films were fourth for women, fifteen percent, but equal second for men, twenty-eight percent. Cartoons were next for both men and women with four percent, but horror, comedy and crime stories got no result at all for either sex. Neither men nor women chose these types of film as their favourite.

Closure

Ask students to react to the information in the survey: *Which result do you think is the most surprising? Do you think the results would be the same for people in your country?*, etc.

Lesson 3: Speaking

diphthongs

1	2
crime	play
find	paint
write	painter
sci-fi	painting
	say

Follow this procedure in each case.

1 Say a word from each pair several times, e.g., *art – act*. Do not let students say anything.
2 Isolate the vowel sounds. Do not let students say anything.
3 Say each pair of stressed vowels for students to repeat chorally.
4 Say each pair of vowels for individual students to repeat.
5 Write the pair of words on the board, in a column marked *1* or *2* (see the tables).
6 Say the vowel sound of one of the two words from the pair. Students must say *1* or *2*.
7 As you do more and more pairs, go back over the previous pairs until you are saying sounds from random from the whole set.

Introduction

Revise the main vowel sounds with words connected with art and literature, plus related verbs.

Write some, or all, of the pairs of letters in the table opposite. Ask students to put as many vowel sounds as possible between the pairs of letters. Most make a real English word, although it does not matter what it means.

long vs short
(based on the stressed syllable in each case)

1	2
art	(act)
drama	(actor)
speak	fiction
feel	literature
	film
story	horror
draw	historical
saw	
talk	
autobiography	
cartoon	comedy
	novel
heard	adventure

( ) = not formally presented in this course

b...d	h...t	p...k	r...m
bad	hat	pack	ram
bard	heart	park	–
bid	hit	pick	rim
bead	heat	peek	ream
bed	het	peck	rem
bird	hurt	perk	–
bod	hot	pock	rom
bored	haught(y)	–	–
bud	hut	puck	rum
booed	hoot	–	room
buoyed	–	–	–
bowed /əʊ/	–	poke	roam
bowed /aʊ/	–	–	–
beard	–	–	–
bide	height	pike	rhyme
bayed	hate	–	–

Exercise A

Give students plenty of time to study the pictures and work out what they show.

1   Set for pairwork. Feed back.

2   Set for pairwork. Make sure students realize that they have to use the genre word, not the letter, e.g., *The historical film is probably a drama.* Give some language for students to use, e.g., *I don't think the crime story is a drama. I agree, but the historical film is probably a drama.* Feed back.

Answers

1   A Crime
    B Adventure – some students may name this as Historical, too.
    C Science fiction
    D Cartoon
    E Horror
    F Love story
    G Comedy
    H Historical

2   Possibly B, F and H.

Exercise B

Make sure students are ready, as you can only usefully play the sounds once. Ask students to put up their hands when they can name the type of film, but not to speak. Ideally, all or most hands should shoot up at the first strains. Invite students to name the event – do not accept the letter of the picture as an answer.

Answers

Possible answers:

1   a comedy
2   a crime film
3   a horror film
4   a cartoon
5   a love story
6   a science fiction film
7   an adventure film
8   a historical film

Tapescript

Presenter: Lesson 3
             B Listen. Which type of film?
             Music that would be used to
             accompany:
             1 a comedy
             2 a crime film
             3 a horror film
             4 a cartoon
             5 a love story
             6 a science fiction film
             7 an adventure film
             8 a historical film

Language and culture note

Are the associations between music and types of film/story ethnocentric? In other words, is there something universal about them, or do they belong to one culture? The writer would be interested to hear how this exercise works with different cultures.

Exercise C

Refer students to the film posters again.

1   Set for individual work and pairwork checking. Do not allow students to shout out. Ask them to listen, identify the film, then check their ideas with a partner each time. Pause after each description for students to discuss. Do not feed back at this point.

2   Set for pairwork. Feed back orally. Allow students to struggle a bit with the use of words, correcting each other, ideally, but eventually model a correct answer.

Answers

1   1   H
    2   D
    3   A
    4   C

2   Depend on the students.

Methodology note

Exercise C2 is a deep-end strategy activity, to see how much of the form as opposed to the content students have actually heard while focusing on the content.

Tapescript

Presenter: **C 1   Listen. Which film is each person talking about?**

Voices: 1   I think this film is about a very brave pilot. His plane catches fire and he finds himself in danger. He probably has lots of adventures.

2   I think this film is about four animals. It is probably set in the present time. The four animals are probably friends and they have lots of adventures. In the end, they probably live happily ever after.

3   I think this film is about a murder. It is probably set in the 1930s. Perhaps a private detective tries to find the murderer. In the end, he probably shoots the murderer.

4   I think this film is about a visit to another planet. It is probably set in the future – perhaps the 25th century. A spaceship lands on the planet and the crew meet the strange people who live there. At the end, they probably return to the Earth. Perhaps they bring one of the people with them.

Methodology note

This is principally a speaking lesson. The listening passages here are partly to revise identifying target vocabulary in the stream of speech, but mainly to provide models for the next speaking activity.

Exercise D

Give students time to read the Skills Check. Point out the different ways you can change a fact to a possibility. Drill the sentences, giving facts, then a word to go into the sentence, e.g.,

You say: *The love story is set in 1800. (think)*
Students say: *I think the love story is set in 1800.*
You say: *They get married at the end. (probably)*
Students say: *They probably get married at the end.*, etc.

Point out that, as so often with the verb *be*, the position of the adverb is different, i.e., after *is*, but before other verbs.

Note that you can combine two points to reduce the possibility further, e.g., *I think perhaps the love story is set in 1800.* But some combinations do not work, e.g., *perhaps + possibly.*

Exercise E

Refer students to the four example answers in the speech bubbles.

Elicit sentences about film E from a good student, then set for pairwork. Monitor and assist. Feed back, getting students to say some of the good guesses – in terms of content as well as form – to the whole class.

Methodology note

Give students some more language in case they cannot work out anything, e.g.,
> *It's difficult to say.*
> *I'm not sure.*
> *I can't tell.*

Methodology note

Activating schemata is a vital part of comprehension. If we are not ready for the kind of information we are going to hear, or read, we may not understand it. We use pictures and other cues to activate words, structures and scenarios when we listen or read in our first language. We must check, with an activity of this kind, that our students are able to activate schemata in English.

Exercise F

Elicit answers from individual students, or set for pairwork, then elicit.

Closure

Make sure students can say the names of the genres with reasonable accuracy and with the correct stress as follows:

First syllable:
'horror
'comedy
'science
'fiction

Second syllable:
ad'venture
his'torical
car'toon

Lesson 4: Speaking

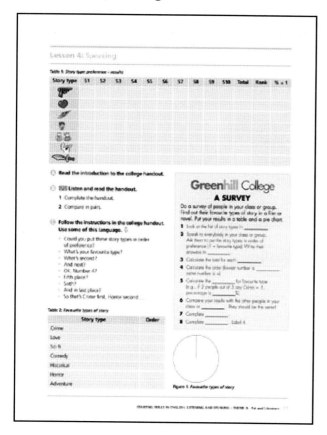

Introduction

Remind students about the verbs from Lesson 2. Mime some for students to name. Elicit the infinitive at this point.

Tell a story with a lot of action and elicit the past tense forms, e.g.,

The man was behind me. I looked at him. He put his hand in his pocket. He brought out a gun. He pointed it at me. I ran. I climbed a wall. I jumped down. I found a door. I opened it. I went in. I closed the door. I got chairs and tables. I carried them into the room. I built/made a barricade. (Do not worry about the word *barricade* – just mime it!)

Exercise A

Set for individual work. Do some quick comprehension questions on the first paragraph.

Exercise B

Set for individual work and pairwork checking. Play the tape, pausing if necessary after target information.

Answers

1 Look at the list of story types in *Table 1*.
2 Speak to everybody in your class or group. Ask them to put the story types in order of preference (*1* = favourite type). Write their answers in *Table 1*.
3 Calculate the total for each *student*.
4 Calculate the order (lowest number is *1*, same number is =).
5 Calculate the *percentage* for favourite type (e.g., if 2 people out of 5 say Crime = *1*, percentage is *40%*).
6 Compare your results with the other people in your class or *group*. They should be the same!
7 Complete *Table 2*.
8 Complete *Figure 1*. Label it.

Tapescript

Presenter:	**Lesson 4**	
	B Listen and read the handout.	
Voice:	1	Look at the list of story types in [PAUSE] Table 1.
	2	Speak to everybody in your class or group. Ask them to put the story types in order of preference (*one* equals favourite type). Write their answers in [PAUSE] Table 1.
	3	Calculate the total for each [PAUSE] student.
	4	Calculate the order (the lowest number is [PAUSE] *one*, the same number is *equals*.)

5 Calculate the [PAUSE] percentage for favourite type, for example, if two people out of five say Crime, that equals one, the percentage is [PAUSE] forty percent.

6 Compare your results with the other people in your class or [PAUSE] group. They should be the same!

7 Complete [PAUSE] Table 2.

8 Complete [PAUSE] Figure 1. Label it.

Methodology note

Students may need further help with understanding the instructions for the survey. If so, you could show the following completed Table 1, plus results table and figure.

Table 1: *Story type preference – results*

Story type	S1	S2	S3	S4	S5	Total	Rank	% = 1	Notes
Crime	1	6	1	2	1	11	1	60%	3 out of 5
Love	2	5	3	4	7	21	4		
Science fiction	3	4	7	3	6	23	= 5		
Comedy	4	7	2	5	5	23	= 5		
Historical	5	1	4	6	4	20	3	20%	1 out of 5
Horror	6	2	6	7	3	24	7		
Adventure	7	3	5	1	2	18	2	20%	1 out of 5

Table 2: *Favourite types of story*

Story type	Order
Crime	1
Love	4
Science fiction	= 5
Comedy	= 5
Historical	3
Horror	7
Adventure	2

Figure 1: *Favourite types of story*

Methodology note

Ideally, one would redo Table 2 in the order of preference, e.g.,

Story type	Order
Crime	1
Adventure	2
Historical	3
Love	4
Science fiction	= 5
Comedy	= 5
Horror	7

The reason this is not done here is because students have not formally learnt the spelling of these words. However, you might like to do this on the board at the end, having collected together the results of the whole class. There is no number 6 as there are equals 5s.

Exercise C

Put students into groups, ideally of ten in order to make the mathematics easy later. If you have a mixed gender group, put the students into groups of male and female so that you can compare the results by gender at the end. Model the sentences by going through the task of eliciting order of preference from a good student. Drill some of the sentences.

Monitor and assist throughout the activity, lock-stepping students through the points on the college handout and making sure that everything is being done correctly by all groups.

Methodology note

Clearly, as it says in number 6 on the handout, Table 1 information should be the same. Make sure students do this point and correct any errors. They might like to hear the columns in Table 1 with the initials of the respondent so they can double-check that students were giving the same answer each time.

Closure

Feed back, getting groups to give their results.

Make a composite table and pie chart with the total results for the whole class. Display it.

General note

By the end of this theme, students should be able to hear and identify, in isolation and in context, the following words linked with TV programmes. They should also be able to say them with reasonable pronunciation, especially stress in multi-syllable words, and use them in simple S V O V and S V O A sentences.

comedy	music	show
documentary	news	soap
film	newspaper	sports
game	opera	talk
hobby	programme	

They should also be able to identify, in isolation and in context, the following verbs, in the present and the past, simple and continuous.

turn off
turn on

In the listening activities in Lesson 2, there are two structure points which have not been formally dealt with to date:

1 *make* + object + verb or adjective (*-ed*)
2 *find* + object + adjective (*-ing*)

This is for comprehension and unanalyzed production at this stage. The structures are analyzed and practised in Lesson 3: Speaking, and later in *Vocabulary and Grammar*.

Lesson 1: Listening

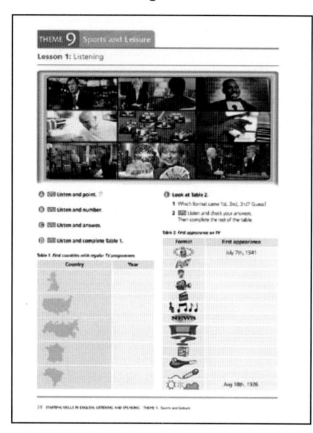

1   activity + place
    Possible pairs:

shopping	mall
play	theatre
film	cinema
sport	stadium
surfing/swimming	sea/beach

2   Say the first half of a common pair and see if
    students can complete the semi-fixed phrase.
    Possible phrases:

radio and	television
films and	plays
football and	tennis
sports and	leisure

Then put some, or all, of the words into sentence
context.

Introduction

Students may already be familiar with the following
words from this lexical set:

ball	shopping
beach	sport
cinema	stadium
film	surfing
football	swimming
leisure	television
mall	tennis
music	theatre
play	watch
radio	

If you are in any doubt, check that all the students can
identify and produce these words in isolation. Check or
teach the related words.

Exercise A

Make sure students realize that all the pictures show
television programmes. Give students plenty of time to
look at all the pictures. Play the tape.

Tapescript

Presenter: Theme 9 Sports and Leisure
             Lesson 1
             A Listen and point.
Voice: news
             sports programme
             music programme
             comedy show
             talk show
             game show
             hobby programme
             documentary
             soap opera

Voice: Did you see the documentary last night about the *Titanic*?

I can't bear game shows. I find them annoying.

There are so many hobby programmes on television now – gardening, cookery, fashion, travel.

I watch the news every night, usually on cable.

There aren't many good music programmes on TV in my country, except MTV.

I love all the soap operas. I don't know why. They're very silly, but I never miss them.

Do you like that new comedy show on Channel 6? It didn't make me laugh at all.

There are too many sports programmes. Every time you turn on – football, tennis, golf. I never watch any of them.

I quite like some of the talk shows, when they get interesting people on.

Methodology note

It is possible that some words here will be completely new to students. Do not try to explain these words at this point. Just make sure that they are associating the word or phrase with the correct picture. Exercise B explains the different types of programme.

Language and culture note

Some types of TV programme seem to collocate with the word *programme*, some with *show*, and some stand alone. This is not directly addressed until *Vocabulary and Grammar* for this theme.

	Stands alone	Programme	Show
news	✓		
documentary	✓	✓	
sports		✓	
music		✓	✓
hobby		✓	
comedy	✓	✓	✓
talk/chat			✓
game			✓

Exercise B

Explain that students are going to hear a definition of each type of TV programme. They should make a prediction about the type of programme as soon as possible, but not shout out. Encourage them to write a number beside a picture in pencil, then change it if necessary as they get more information. Play the tape, pausing after each passage.

Answers

1	This programme is on every night. They tell you the events of the day – the good things, but mostly the bad things. There is usually information about accidents, crimes and fighting in some part of the world.	*news*
2	There are two types of programme. Sometimes people just talk about the next game, but usually there is live sport.	*sports programme*
3	The format is simple. One person or a group stands up and plays music. Perhaps there is an interview with the person or the group before or after the music.	*music programme*

4	Sometimes a person stands up and tells jokes, but the most common type of programme is a short play with a funny situation.	*comedy show*
5	There are two main types. Sometimes a person talks to famous people, sometimes ordinary people are on the show. In one kind of show, people bring their problems and try to solve them.	*talk show*
6	There are many types but they all have the same basic format. One person asks questions and another person or a group of people try to answer them. At the end, the person or people may win a prize.	*game show*
7	These programmes tell people how to do something – gardening, cookery, travel, Do-It-Yourself, fashion, collecting of various sorts.	*hobby programme*
8	This type of programme is about real people and real events. Sometimes there is film from the past, sometimes just pictures. There are usually interviews with people involved in the events, or with scientists or researchers.	*documentary*
9	This kind of programme has a strange name. The format is always the same. We see the ordinary lives of a group of people from the same family or the same village, town or city. But the lives are not always ordinary. There are many problems for the people, and, often, there are crimes.	*soap opera*

Tapescript

Presenter: **B Listen and number.**

Voice: 1 This programme is on every night. They tell you the events of the day, the good things, but mostly the bad things. There is usually information about accidents, crimes and fighting in some part of the world.

2 There are two types of programme. Sometimes people just talk about the next game, but usually there is live sport.

3 The format is simple. One person or a group stands up and plays music. Perhaps there is an interview with the person or the group before or after the music.

4 Sometimes a person stands up and tells jokes, but the most common type of programme is a short play with a funny situation.

5 There are two main types. Sometimes a person talks to famous people, sometimes ordinary people are on the show. In one kind of show, people bring their problems and try to solve them.

6 There are many types but they all have the same basic format. One person asks questions and another person or a group of people try to answer them. At the end, the person or people may win a prize.

7 These programmes tell people how to do something – gardening, cookery, travel, Do-It-Yourself, fashion, collecting of various sorts.

8 This type of programme is about real people and real events. Sometimes there is film from the past, sometimes just pictures. There are usually interviews with people involved in the events, or with scientists or researchers.

9 This kind of programme has a strange name. The format is always the same. We see the ordinary lives of a group of people from the same family or the same village, town or city. But the lives are not always ordinary. There are many problems for the people, and, often, there are crimes.

Exercise C

Remind students of the two kinds of questions. Say or play the first two as examples. Elicit answers. Point out or demonstrate the fall-rise at the end of *Yes/No* questions, and the high start of the information questions. Play the remaining questions, pausing after each one for students to think of an answer, then nominating one student to answer.

Answers

Questions with possible answers:

1	Is news on TV every night in your country?	*Yes, it is.*
2	What sort of information do you get in a news programme?	*Information about the events of the day.*
3	What is live sport?	*Sport happening now.*
4	Do you ever get interviews in a music programme?	*Yes, you do. Sometimes.*
5	What do you call programmes which make you laugh?	*Comedy programmes/shows.*
6	Do people usually win prizes on quiz shows?	*Yes, they do.*
7	What sort of programme often has famous people on it?	*Talk shows.*
8	What sort of information do you get on a hobby programme?	*How to do something in your leisure time.*
9	What's the difference between the news and a documentary?	*News is happening now, but a documentary is about events in the past or present.*
10	Is a soap opera about soap?	*No, it isn't. It's about people living their normal lives.*
11	Do you turn on the television when you get home?	*Answers depend on the students.*
12	What time do you turn off the television at night?	*Answers depend on the students.*

Tapescript

Presenter: C Listen and answer.

Voice:
1 Is news on TV every night in your country?
2 What sort of information do you get in a news programme?
3 What is live sport?
4 Do you ever get interviews in a music programme?
5 What do you call programmes which make you laugh?
6 Do people usually win prizes on quiz shows?
7 What sort of programme often has famous people on it?
8 What sort of information do you get on a hobby programme?
9 What's the difference between the news and a documentary?
10 Is a soap opera about soap?
11 Do you turn on the television when you get home?
12 What time do you turn off the television at night?

Language and culture note

This is a deep-end strategy activity. Students may struggle to answer the questions. Allow them to help each other to come up with a suitable answer in each case.

Exercise D

Ask students *Which country had regular TV programmes first?* Explain the word *regular* as *every day*. Elicit ideas, but do not confirm or correct. Refer students to Table 1. Ask them if they can identify any of the countries. Once again, do not confirm or correct. Set for individual work and pairwork checking. Play the tape. Feed back, eliciting the names of the countries in order.

Answers

Country	Year
UK	1936
USA	1939
USSR	1939
France	1948
Brazil	1950

Tapescript

Presenter: D Listen and complete Table 1.

Voice: There were televisions in the UK, in the USA and in Germany from the 1920s, but the first country to have regular TV programmes was the UK. The service started in 1936. Regular programmes began in the USA three years later, in 1939. In the same year, regular broadcasts began in the USSR. This was the name of Russia at that time. The Second World War, from 1939 to 1945, stopped the spread of regular TV broadcasts, but in 1948, they started in France. Two years later, Brazil started a regular TV service.

Exercise E

1 Refer students to Table 2. Ask them to discuss in pairs. Elicit, but do not confirm or correct.
2 Set for individual work and pairwork checking. Play the first part of the tape. Feed back, eliciting the correct order and the dates.

Set the second part of the activity for individual work and pairwork checking. Play the rest of the tape. Feed back, ideally onto an OHT of Table 2.

Answers

1, 2 weather map
   music show
   talk show

Format	First appearance
advertisement	July 7th, 1941
cartoon	*July 7th, 1941*
comedy show	*Oct 11th, 1949*
documentary	*Nov 18th, 1951*
film	*May 31st, 1938*
music show	*1928*
news	*May 2nd, 1944*
play	*Sept 11th, 1928*
quiz show	*Feb 28th, 1940*
soap opera	*Oct 2nd, 1946*
sports programme	*July 12th, 1928*
talk show	*1928*
weather map	Aug 18th, 1926

Tapescript

Presenter: **E 2 Listen and check your answers. Then complete the rest of the table.**

Part 1

Voice: Regular TV broadcasts started in the UK in 1936 and in the USA in 1939. But long before that, there were a small number of television programmes. For example, the first weather map appeared on television on August 18th, 1926. Perhaps this was the first ever real TV programme. In 1928, some television stations made music shows and, shortly after, talk shows.

Part 2

Voice: The first live sports programme appeared on July 12th, 1928. It was a tennis match. The first play appeared a few months later, on September 11th, 1928. It was called *The Queen's Messenger*. It was a long time before television stations produced a new kind of programme. The first film appeared on May 31st, 1938. The title of the film was *The Return of the Scarlet Pimpernel*. The first quiz show

appeared two years later, on February 28th, 1940. It was a spelling quiz. The first advertisement on TV, for watches, appeared on July 7th, 1941, and on the same day, people watched the first cartoon. It was the children's story *Jack and the Beanstalk*. Most people are surprised to find out that the first news broadcast did not appear until 1944, May 2nd of that year. The first soap opera appeared on October 2nd, 1946. It was called *Faraway Hill*. The name *soap opera* comes from the advertisements in the middle of the programme. They were advertisements for soap powder. Not soap for washing yourself. Soap for washing clothes. Another surprise is the first comedy show on television. It did not appear until October 11th, 1949. Finally, the documentary. The first documentary appeared on November 18th, 1951.

Methodology notes

1 The word *format* appears in the table, but it is not necessary to dwell on it. It should be clear from the contents of the column that it means 'type of programme'. Students must be taught to tolerate ambiguity in this way, i.e., *I have not been taught this, but I can work it out.*
2 This is revision of identifying and reproducing full dates.

Closure

Ask students mixed questions about the table. See if they can identify perfectly the two types of question, and answer them with the correct information and correct forms.

Lesson 2: Listening

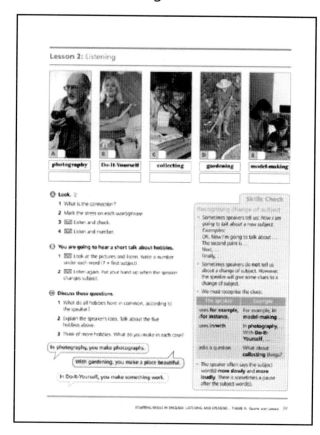

Introduction

Say the stressed syllable of the key multi-syllable words from Lesson 1. Students identify the full word.

ho	*hobby*
com /kʌm/	*comedy*
pro /prəʊ/	*programme*
mu	*music*
men	*documentary*
soa /səʊ/	*soap opera*

Methodology note

This is still recognition. Do not worry about pronunciation of target words, as long as they are recognizable.

Exercise A

1   Refer students to the pictures. Give students time to look at all of them. Ask the question and elicit answers. Confirm. They are all hobbies.
2   Students will have to guess where the stress lies, so suggest they work in pencil.
3   Play the tape. Feed back, getting the words on the board with the correct stress.
4   Play the tape again. Ask students to number the pictures.

Answers

1   They are all hobbies.
2, 3   pho'tography
  Do-It-Your'self
  co'llecting
  'gardening
  'model-making
4 1 D gardening
  2 A photography
  3 E model-making
  4 C collecting
  5 B Do-It-Yourself

Tapescript

Presenter: Lesson 2
    A 3 Listen and check.
Voice: pho'tography
   Do-It-Your'self
   co'llecting
   'gardening
   'model-making

Presenter: **A 4 Listen and number.**
Voice: 1 I like gardens, but I don't actually like gardening.
   2 Millions of people are now interested in photography.
   3 I think everyone has done some model-making at one time in their lives.

4 People like collecting all sorts of things – coins, stamps, postcards, even car numbers.

5 There's a Do-It-Yourself shop in every major town in Britain.

Language and culture note

Students may well get the stress wrong on the first three. In particular, the more common word, 'photograph, has a different stress from the abstract noun. Point this out in the feedback.

Exercise B

Explain that students are going to hear a short talk about the items in the pictures. They must number the items in the order they are talked about. They will not actually hear any numbers. But if the speaker talks about photography first, they should mark that.

1 Set for individual work and pairwork checking. Do not feed back at this point.

2 Set for individual work. Play the tape again, pausing when a significant number of students have put up their hands. Review what the speaker has just said.

Answers

A 2
B 3
C 5
D 4
E 1

Tapescript

Presenter: B 1 Look at the pictures and listen. Write a number under each word. One equals first subject.

Voice: A hobby is something you do in your leisure time. There are many different hobbies in the world, but they have one thing in common. Every hobby involves making something. Sometimes it is easy to see the result of the hobby.

For example, in model-making, [PAUSE] there is a model at the end. But many people get more enjoyment from making the model than from looking at it or playing with it.

In photography, [PAUSE] there is, of course, a photograph, although nowadays, with digital photography, the picture is sometimes deleted and never printed.

Sometimes, with Do-It-Yourself [PAUSE] there is a clear result. People make things, like tables and cupboards. But most Do-It-Yourself is just repairing something – plumbing, electrical work – or simply painting a room. You are still making something, though. You are making the tap work, or the lights work, or you are making the room look nicer.

Gardening [PAUSE] is similar to Do-It-Yourself. You make a space look more beautiful.

But what about collecting? [PAUSE] What are you making in this case? Stamp collectors don't make stamps, coin collectors don't make coins. But they do make something. They make a collection. They put their stamps, for example, in a big book, in alphabetical order of country.

Presenter: B 2 Listen again. Put your hand
                up when the speaker changes
                subject.
                [REPEAT OF EXERCISE B1]

Methodology note

On this occasion, students are allowed to hear the
tape for a second time. As you know, the basic
methodology of the *Starting Skills in English* series
is that students should hear spoken language once
only, as this mimics real life. Here, it is useful to
allow them to hear the tape again so you can see if
they are really sensing the change of subject.

Exercise C

Set for pairwork or groupwork. Monitor and assist,
especially with the structure *make* + object (+ verb/
adjective). Refer students to the speech bubbles if they
get stuck with this structure. Feed back orally.

Answers
Possible answers:

1   They all involve making something.
2   Students should be able to remember some of the
    ideas from the talk.
3   Answers depend on the students, but if they say
    things like *reading*, point out that this is an interest
    rather than a hobby because it does not involve
    making things.

Closure

Get students to identify key words from this lesson and
Lesson 1 from the stressed syllable.

Lesson 3: Speaking

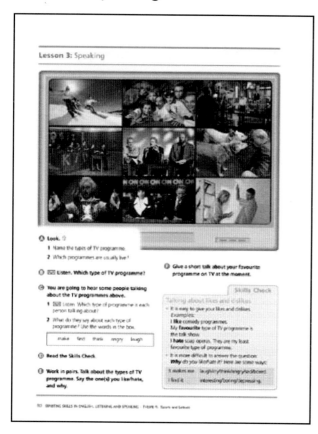

Introduction

Revise the main vowel sounds with words connected with sports and leisure.

long vs short
(based on the stressed syllable in each case)

1	2
gardening	(stamp)
TV	film
	quiz
sports	photography
mall	model
cartoon	comedy
news	
music	
person	documentary
turn (on/off)	collecting
	leisure
talk	watch hobby
	shopping opera

( ) = not formally presented in this course

diphthongs

1	2
(prize)	play
	make
	radio
show	about
soap	
(joke)	
programme	

Follow this procedure in each case.

1. Say a word from each pair several times, e.g., *gardening – stamp*. Do not let students say anything.
2. Isolate the vowel sounds. Do not let students say anything.
3. Say each pair of stressed vowels for students to repeat chorally.
4. Say each pair of vowels for individual students to repeat.
5. Write the pair of words on the board, in a column marked *1* or *2* (see the tables).
6. Say the vowel sound of one of the two words from the pair. Students must say *1* or *2*.
7. As you do more and more pairs, go back over the previous pairs until you are saying sounds from random from the whole set.

Say a vowel sound and ask students to think of words with that sound. Here are the sounds you must make (contained in a word as an example).

1	2
bad	bard
bed	bird
bid	bead
bod	board
bud	booed
book	

bake	bike	
boat	bout	
boil		
tier	tear	tour

Exercise A

Give students plenty of time to study the TV screens and work out what they show.
1   Set for pairwork. Feed back.
2   Set for pairwork. Make sure students realize that they have to use the name of the programme-type word, not the letter, e.g., *The talk show is probably live.* Give some language for students to use, e.g., *I don't think the documentary is live. I agree, but the music show may be live.* Feed back.

Answers
1   Row 1:
    sports programme
    comedy show
    soap opera

    Row 2:
    quiz show
    talk show
    documentary

    Row 3:
    music show
    news
    hobby programme/Do-It-Yourself programme
2   Possibly the sports programme, the talk show, the music show and the news are live.

Exercise B

Make sure students are ready, as you can only usefully play the sounds once. Ask students to put up their hands when they can name the type of programme, but not to speak. Ideally, all or most hands should shoot up at the first strains. Invite students to name the type of programme.

Answers
Possible answers:

1   a comedy programme
2   an opera
3   the news
4   a quiz show
5   a soap
6   a sports event
7   a talk show
8   a documentary
9   a DIY programme

Tapescript

Presenter:	Lesson 3
	B Listen. Which type of TV programme?
Sound effects:	1 a comedy programme
	2 an opera
	3 the news
	4 a quiz show
	5 a soap opera
	6 a sports event
	7 a talk show
	8 a documentary
	9 an extract from a DIY programme

Exercise C

Refer students to the TV screens again.
1   Set for individual work and pairwork checking. Do not allow students to shout out. Ask them to listen, identify the TV programme, then check their ideas with a partner each time. Pause after each description for students to discuss. Do not feed back at this point.
2   Set for pairwork. Feed back orally. Allow students to struggle a bit with the use of words, correcting each other, ideally, but eventually model a correct answer.

Answers

1   1 a quiz
     2 a sports programme
     3 the news
     4 a talk show
     5 a comedy programme/show
     6 a documentary
2   Depend on the students.

Methodology note

Exercise C2 is a deep-end strategy, to see how much of the form as opposed to the content students have actually heard while focusing on the content.

Tapescript

Presenter: **C 1 Listen. Which type of programme is each person talking about?**

Voice 1:   I quite like this kind of programme. I find the questions very interesting. They make you think. Sometimes I feel stupid because I get a simple one wrong, but I feel very clever when I get it right, and the contestant gets it wrong.

Voice 2:   I hate this kind of programme. They are on all the time and I find them so boring! I want to watch a documentary or a talk show and my brothers turn over to watch a football match or a tennis game.

Voice 3:   I watch it every evening although I find it depressing. You've got to know about the events in the world, though, haven't you?

Voice 4:   I love this kind of programme. Well, at least I love the ones with famous people. I find it interesting when they talk about their lives and their latest film or book. I don't like the ones with ordinary people. They make me angry. I hate all the shouting and the rude words. I turn the sound down, or sometimes, I turn it off altogether.

Voice 5:   There are some good ones on television, but most of them are not really funny. They don't make me laugh at all. I sit there with a smile on my face, but I never actually laugh.

Voice 6:   I really like this kind of programme, especially the ones about nature or animals. My favourite is called *Violent Planet* and it's about all the terrible kinds of weather they get in different countries. I find it really interesting, but it makes me glad to live here!

Methodology note

This is principally a speaking lesson. The listening passages here are partly to revise identifying target vocabulary in the stream of speech, but mainly to provide models for the next speaking activity.

Exercise D

Give students time to read the Skills Check. Point out the different ways you can change expressing likes and dislikes, then ways to explain. Drill the sentences. Highlight the fact that *make* can be used with an object and a verb, or an object and an adjective, but *find* can only be used with an object and an adjective. In addition, you use *-ing* adjectives with *find*, but *-ed* adjectives with *make*. Get students to convert from one kind of sentence to another, e.g.,

You say: *It makes me bored. (interesting)*
Students say: *I find it interesting.*

Methodology note

Students probably do not really know enough *-ed-/-ing*-type adjectives to fully exploit this now, so you may wish to quickly check or teach the following:

> *interested/interesting*
> *bored/boring*
> *frightened/frightening*
> *excited/exciting*

Teach the following as alternatives to known words:

> *depressed/depressing* instead of *sad*
> *amused/amusing* instead of *funny*
> *annoyed/annoying* instead of *angry*

Exercise E

Elicit sentences about two of the types of programmes from good students, then set for pairwork. Monitor and assist. Feed back, getting students to say some of the good explanations – in terms of content as well as form – to the whole class.

Methodology note

Give students some more language in case they cannot work out anything, e.g.,

> *It's difficult to say.*
> *I don't really know why.*
> *I can't explain.*
> *I just do.*

Exercise F

Run together some sentences about one of the TV types and give your own personal talk, using some of the patterns from this lesson. Set for individual work and pairwork checking. Monitor and assist.

Closure

Get a few students to give a short personal talk about their favourite or least favourite type of TV programme.

Lesson 4: Speaking

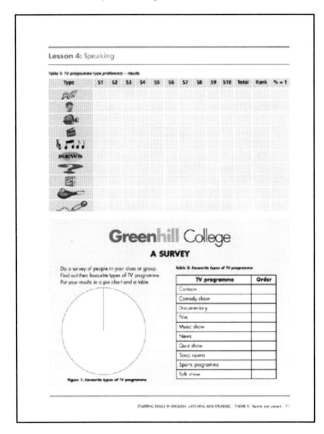

5   Calculate the percentage for favourite type (e.g., if two people out of five say soap operas = *1*, percentage is *40%*).

6   Compare your results with the other people in your class or group. They should be the same!

7   Complete Table 2.

9   Complete Figure 1. Label it.

Methodology note

Students may need further help with understanding the instructions for the survey. If so, you could show completed Table 1, plus the results table and figure.

Closure

Feed back, getting groups to give their results.

Make a composite table and pie chart with the total results for the whole class. Display it.

Introduction

Begin a sentence and get students to finish it in as many ways as they can, e.g.,

> *Quiz shows make me … laugh / scream at the TV / cry / feel stupid.*
> *I find the news … boring / interesting / frightening / is the same every day.*

For the whole of this lesson, follow the procedure from Lesson 4 of Theme 8.

Elicit the procedure for a survey from the students, i.e.,

1   Look at the list of types of TV programmes in Table 1.

2   Speak to everybody in your class or group. Ask them to put the types in order of preference (*1* = favourite type). Write their answers in Table 1.

3   Calculate the total for each student.

4   Calculate the order (lowest number is *1*, same number is =).

General notes

This is a revision theme in terms of skills.

During Lessons 1 and 2, the majority of the following skills points will be directly or indirectly revised:

- **End focus:** important words are often at the end of sentences
- **Examples and lists:** speakers often use a word or phrase, then give an example
- **Guessing meanings:** from other words in the text
- **Guessing pronunciation:** say new words in your head
- **Guessing spelling:** consonant sounds usually have one common spelling, vowel sounds can have many spellings
- **Identifying multi-syllable words from the strong sound**
- **Identifying questions:** *do / did / is / are / was / were* or *when / where / who / what*
- **Listening and reacting:** when speakers give you alternatives, think *Which is the best way?*
- **Joining words and prediction:** understanding the value of *and*, *but*, or *or*
- **Predicting the content of a talk:** what is the lecturer going to talk about/say next?
- **Predicting the structure of a talk:** speakers sometimes help us to predict the structure of a talk
- **Recognizing change of subject**
- **Using the correct short form:** listen to the form at the start of a *Yes/No* question, and use it in your answer

During Lessons 3 and 4, some of the following skills points will be directly or indirectly revised:

- **Answering questions:** answer information questions with information, and *Yes/No* questions with *Yes* or *No* + S + *am/have* (*not*)
- **Asking about regular events:** *usually, ever, often*
- **Asking about the weather**
- **Comparing notes:** names and numbers
- **Comparing two things:** *Most German children study English, but most Australian children study Japanese.*
- **Improving your pronunciation:** identifying difficult sounds, checking the stress
- **Starting a conversation (1):** leaving words out, i.e., *It's, It's a, What a*
- **Starting a conversation (2):** talking about travel
- **Stressing long words:** most words with 2 or 3 syllables have the stress on the first syllable
- **Talking about likes and dislikes:** *I quite like history. Do you? I do, too.*
- **Talking about possibilities:** changing fact into a possibility
- **Talking about quantity:** *All children study ..., 10% of children study ...*
- **Talking about reasons for likes and dislikes:** answering the question *Why?*
- **Talking about regular events:** frequency adverbs
- **Talking about the weather:** different patterns with different weather words
- **Talking about the past with *ago*:** time period + *ago*

By the end of this theme, students should be able to hear and identify, in isolation and in context, the following words linked with food and drink items and their packaging. They should also be able to say them with reasonable pronunciation, especially stress in multi-syllable words, and use them in simple S V (O) (C) sentences.

bottle	cup	pepper
bowl	glass	restaurant
breakfast	jam	salt
can	meal	
carton	menu	

Lesson 1: Listening

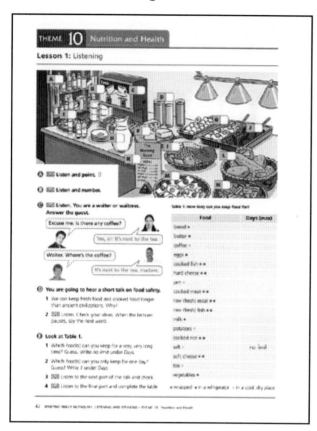

hot drinks	coffee
	tea
cold drinks	juice
	water
	milk
meat	chicken
salad	vegetables
food	bread
	butter, etc.

2 Then give a group word/phrase and elicit a member, then vice versa.

Then put some or all of the words into sentence context.

Exercise A

Refer students to the picture. Elicit that this is *breakfast*. Give students plenty of time to look at everything in the picture. Play the tape of the words in isolation. Explain that for the sentences, this time they are going to hear pairs of words that commonly go together. They must point to both items in the pair. Play the first one as an example.

Tapescript

Presenter:	Theme 10 Nutrition and Health
	Lesson 1
	A Listen and point.
Voice:	bread
	butter
	cheese
	coffee
	eggs
	fruit
	juice
	milk
	potatoes
	sugar
	tea
	water
	salt
	pepper

Introduction

Students may already be familiar with the following words from this lexical set:

bread	juice
butter	meat
cheese	milk
chicken	potato
coffee	rice
drink	salad
eat	sandwich
egg	sugar
fish	tea
food	vegetable
fruit	water
ice-cream	

If you are in any doubt, check that all the students can identify and produce these words in isolation.

1 Check or teach the group word, plus members, i.e.,

jam

menu

restaurant

Voice: Can I have some bread and butter, please?

Would you like coffee or tea?

Do you want milk and sugar?

Where's the salt and pepper?

Would you prefer water or juice?

I love bread and jam.

My favourite food is bread and cheese.

Could I see the menu?

What's the name of this restaurant?

Exercise B

Set the situation clearly, perhaps acting out a waiter-guest scenario with a good student. Point out that students must write the number of the table – table in a restaurant, not table of information – next to the items which are ordered. Play the first one up to the order of eggs as an example. Continue with the rest.

Answers

eggs – Table 1

coffee – Tables 1, 4

orange juice – Table 1

tea – Table 2

milk – Table 2

sugar – Table 2

salt – Table 3

pepper – Table 3

Tapescript

Presenter: **B Listen and number.**

Table 1

Waiter: What would you like to eat?

Male guest: I'll have eggs, please. Just eggs.

Waiter: Boiled, scrambled or fried, sir?

Male guest: Fried, please.

Waiter: And what would you like to drink?

Male guest: Coffee, please, no milk or sugar.

Waiter: Certainly, sir. Orange juice?

Male guest: Yes, please.

Presenter: **Table 2**

Waitress: What can I get you, madam?

Female guest: Just tea, please, with milk and sugar.

Waitress: Nothing to eat?

Female guest: Um, let me see. No, thank you.

Presenter: **Table 3**

Male guest: Excuse me.

Waiter: Yes, sir.

Male guest: Can I have the salt and pepper, please?

Waiter: Yes, certainly.

Presenter: **Table 4**

Female guest: More coffee, please.

Waitress: Sorry? More tea?

Female guest: Coffee.

Waitress: Oh, sorry.

Exercise C

Make sure students understand the scenario. Play out one of the two mini-conversations with good students. Make sure students see that there are two types of question. Play the tape. Do not let students shout out the answer. Hold them, then allow one student to respond. Play the tape again, indicating in advance which student should answer each question.

Tapescript

Presenter: C Listen. You are a waiter or waitress. Answer the guest.

Voice: Is there any coffee?

[PAUSE]

Where's the sugar?

[PAUSE]

Is there any milk?

[PAUSE]

Where's the salt?

[PAUSE]

Are there any eggs?

[PAUSE]

Where's the milk?

[PAUSE]

Are there any potatoes?

[PAUSE]

Is there any jam?

[PAUSE]

Have you got any fruit?

[PAUSE]

Do you have apples?

Exercise D

Explain the difference between fresh (raw) food and cooked food. Perhaps use mime.

1   Set for pairwork. Elicit ideas, but do not confirm or correct.
2   Play the tape of the introduction.

Tapescript

Presenter: D 2 Listen. Check your ideas. When the lecturer pauses, say the next word.

Introduction

Lecturer: At one time, people had to use fresh food and cooked food very quickly. They could not keep it for more than [PAUSE] one or two days. But we have two things in our homes to help us keep [PAUSE] fresh food and cooked food. Firstly, we have the [PAUSE] refrigerator. In 1856, an Australian called James Harrison produced the first refrigerator – a box with a constant temperature of around [PAUSE] four degrees centigrade. Secondly, we have [PAUSE] plastic wrapping for food. In 1933, an American called Ralph Wiley discovered PVC. After the Second World War, people began to use it to wrap [PAUSE] fresh food and cooked food. The refrigerator and plastic wrapping mean we can keep fresh food and cooked food for quite a long [PAUSE] time.

Exercise E

Refer students to Table 1. Do not elicit the names of the foods and drinks – this is a listening lesson. Explain *no limit*. Make sure students see the colour coding.

1   Set for pairwork. Elicit, but do not confirm or correct.
2   Repeat the procedure.
3   Set for individual work and pairwork checking. Play the next part of the talk. Feed back, ensuring that students have got the correct information for *1 day* and *no limit*.
4   Play the remainder of the talk.

Feed back, building up the table on the board, or using an OHT or datashow.

Answers

Food	Days (max)
bread	7
butter	7
coffee	*no limit*
eggs	21
cooked fish	1
hard cheese	90
jam	180
cooked meat	1
raw (fresh) meat	3–4
raw (fresh) fish	2
milk	5
potatoes	180
cooked rice	4–5
salt	no limit
soft cheese	7
tea	*no limit*
vegetables	3–4

Tapescript

Presenter: **E 3 Listen to the next part of the talk and check.**

Voice: So how long can we keep fresh food and cooked food for? Well, for some things, there is really no limit, if we keep them in a cool dry place. Salt, for example, and coffee and tea. At the other end of the scale, we can only keep cooked meat and fish for one day, wrapped, in a refrigerator.

Presenter: **E 4 Listen to the final part and complete the table.**

Voice: We can keep fresh meat and fish for longer, two days for fish, three to four days for meat. Vegetables also keep for three to four days, cooked rice keeps a little longer, four to five days. Milk should keep for five days, while bread, butter and soft cheese keep for about a week, seven days. Hard cheese, by the way, is different. It keeps for up to three months, that is, ninety days. Eggs keep in a refrigerator for quite a long time, three weeks, or twenty-one days. Finally, jam and potatoes keep for six months or one hundred and eighty days.

Closure

Ask students mixed questions about the table. See if they can identify perfectly the two types of question, and answer them with the correct information and correct forms.

Lesson 2: Listening

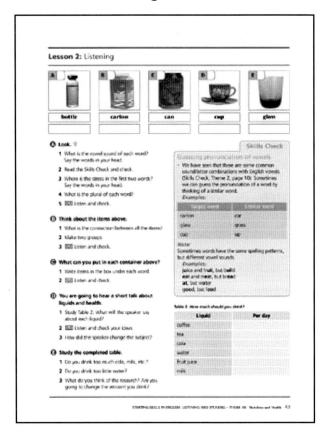

Introduction

Say the stressed syllable of the key multi-syllable words from Lesson 1. Students identify the full word.

bo	*bottle*
break /brek/	*breakfast*
men	*menu*
rest	*restaurant*
sa	*salt*
ta /teɪ/	*potato*
chi	*chicken*
veg	*vegetable*
wa /wɔː/	*water*
su /ʃʊ/	*sugar*
co /kɒ/	*coffee*

Exercise A

1   Refer students to the pictures. Set for individual work and pairwork checking. Do not feed back.
2   Set for individual work and pairwork checking. Do not feed back, but remind students about common vowel sounds for each vowel (Skills Check, Part B, Theme 2). That should help them with two of the sounds – *bottle* and *can*.
3   Repeat the procedure.
4   Play the tape. Feed back, getting students to say the whole words, then each vowel sound in isolation. Drill the words.

Work through the points in the Skills Check.

Answers

'bottle /ɒ/ – bottles
'carton /ɑː/ – cartons
can /æ/ – cans
cup /ʌ/ – cups
glass /ɑː/ – glasses

Tapescript

Presenter:	Lesson 2	
	A 5 Listen and check.	
Voice:	'bottle [PAUSE] 'bottles	
	'carton [PAUSE] 'cartons	
	can [PAUSE] cans	
	cup [PAUSE] cups	
	glass [PAUSE] 'glasses	

Methodology note

This is a listening lesson, but unless you can predict the sound of a word you have seen and not heard, you may not recognize it when you hear it. Similarly, if you think that one spelling pattern only has one sound, you will predict wrongly and wait in vain for /briːd/, /wætə/ and /fʊd/ in a lecture on nutrition and health. Finally, if you are not expecting the plural *s* to make the sound /z/ or /ɪz/, once again you may not identify the word in context.

Exercise B

1 Set for pairwork. Ask the question and elicit answers, but do not confirm or correct.
2 Point out that there is a connection, but there are also two groups here. Repeat the procedure from activity 1.
3 Play the tape. Feed back, eliciting as much of the content of the tapescript as possible.

Answers

1 They are all containers for liquids.
2 You sell things in bottles, cans and cartons.
  You serve things in, and drink things from, glasses and cups.

Tapescript

Presenter: **B 3 Listen and check.**
Voice: Milk, water, juice, coffee and tea are all liquids. That means you must put them in containers to sell them, or serve them in a restaurant. We use some containers to sell liquids. We use bottles, cartons and cans. Bottles are made of glass, cartons are made of plastic, and cans are made of metal. We use different containers to serve liquids in a restaurant. We use cups for hot drinks and glasses for cold drinks.

Language and culture note

In British and American culture, we talk about a *cup* of tea, not a *glass* of tea. This is mainly because tea is served in china, not glass, but it has also become a fixed phrase, even if the container is made of metal or plastic.

Exercise C

1 Set for individual work and pairwork checking.
2 Play the tape. Feed back orally.

Answers

Bottle	Carton	Can	Cup	Glass
milk	milk	soft drinks	coffee	milk
water	fruit juice	fruit juice	tea	fruit juice
				water
				soft drinks

Tapescript

Presenter: **C 2 Listen and check.**
Voice: What can you put in each container in the pictures? In the Western world, we sell milk and water in bottles. We also sell milk in cartons. So we talk about a bottle of milk or a carton of milk, and a bottle of water. We sell soft drinks and fruit juice in cans. We also sell juices in cartons. We serve tea and coffee in cups. We serve milk, fruit juice, water and soft drinks in glasses. Some people drink soft drinks like cola from cans.

Exercise D

1   Set for pairwork. Give students plenty of time to make predictions about each item in Table 2.

2   Explain that they are going to hear a short talk about liquids and health. This time, they must identify the change of subject and move to the correct place in the table to enter the information. Set for individual work and pairwork checking. Play the tape. Feed back, building up the table on the board.

3   Set for pairwork. Elicit some ideas. Then play the tape again, pausing when the speaker changes subject. Review what the speaker has just said.

Answers

2

Liquid	Per day
coffee	*2 cups*
tea	*2 cups*
cola	*1 can*
water	*4–5 glasses*
fruit juice	*1 glass*
milk	*1 glass*

3   • Sometimes the speaker launches straight into a new subject, e.g., *Cola has lots of sugar.*
    • Sometimes the speaker asks a rhetorical question, e.g., *What about **milk**?*
    • Sometimes the speaker asks you to **look at** something new, e.g., *Let's look at **hot drinks**.*
    • The speaker introduces the broad subject of **fruit**, then refines it to **fruit juice.**
    • The speaker uses a sequencer at the end, i.e., *Finally, we come to **water**.*

Tapescript

Presenter: D 2 **Listen and check your ideas.**

Lecturer: How much cola do you drink every day? What about fruit juice, milk, coffee and tea? You probably drink too much of these liquids, according to recent research. Perhaps you drink too much water, too.

Let's look at the latest research by the United States Food and Nutrition Board and others.

Cola [PAUSE] has lots of sugar. Sugar can be bad for you. Drink only one can of cola a day.

Fruit [PAUSE] is very good for you, but fruit juice [PAUSE] in cartons often has lots of sugar, too. Drink only one glass of fruit juice.

What about milk? [PAUSE] Many years ago, everybody thought that milk was very good for you. Now we know that many people can't drink milk. Perhaps two thirds of people in the world feel bad after drinking milk. So perhaps the answer is: *Don't drink milk at all if it makes you feel bad.* If not, drink only one glass a day.

Let's look at hot drinks. [PAUSE] The most popular hot drink in the world is coffee. [PAUSE] Ninety percent of hot drink sales in the USA are coffee. But coffee can be very bad for you. Drink only two cups a day. Tea [PAUSE] is also very popular. Sixty-six percent of hot drink sales in Britain are tea. But tea is very similar to coffee in many ways. So drink only two cups of tea a day.

Finally, we come to water. [PAUSE] Thirty years ago, an American nutritionist, Dr Stare, said *You need six to eight glasses every day.* But he did not mean drink six to eight glasses. He said *You get water in coffee, tea, milk and soft drinks. You also get water from fruit and vegetables.* In fact, you can drink too much water. Some people have died after drinking more than twenty glasses of water. So how much should you drink? The latest research says you should probably drink four to five glasses a day. But remember! This research is from a cool country. The people did not have manual jobs. If you live in a hot country, and if you do a lot of exercise, you need more water.

Exercise E

Set for pairwork. Feed back orally.

Closure

Get students to identify key words from this lesson and Lesson 1 from the stressed syllable.

Lesson 3: Speaking

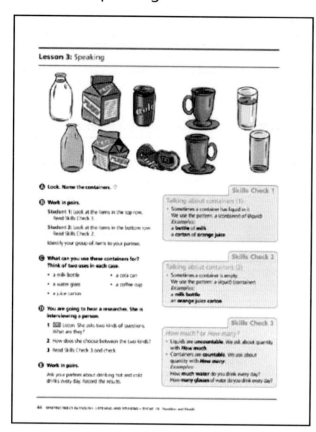

Introduction

Revise the main vowel sounds with words connected with nutrition and health.

long vs short
(based on the stressed syllable in each case)

1	2
glass	salad
carton	sandwich
	can
	jam
cheese	chicken
eat	fish
meat	drink
tea	milk
salt	coffee
water	bottle

1	2
food	cup
juice	
fruit	
sir	menu
(research)	bread
	vegetables
	restaurant

( ) = not formally presented in this course

Follow this procedure in each case.

1 Say a word from each pair several times, e.g., *glass – can*. Do not let students say anything.
2 Isolate the vowel sounds. Do not let students say anything.
3 Say each pair of stressed vowels for students to repeat chorally.
4 Say each pair of vowels for individual students to repeat.
5 Write the pair of words on the board, in a column marked *1* or *2* (see the tables).
6 Say the vowel sound of one of the two words from the pair. Students must say *1* or *2*.
7 As you do more and more pairs, go back over the previous pairs until you are saying sounds from random from the whole set.

Say a vowel sound and ask students to think of words with that sound. Here are the sounds you must make (contained in a word as an example).

1	2
bad	bard
bed	bird
bid	bead
bod	board
bud	booed
book	

Exercise A

Give students plenty of time to study the pictures and work out what they show. Set for pairwork. Feed back. In the feedback, make sure they understand that there are two bottles, two cartons, etc. Do not worry about *full* and *empty* at this point.

Answers
bottle
carton
can
cup
glass

Exercise B

Set for pairwork. Monitor and assist. Feed back. Ask students, e.g.,

> *Where's the bottle of milk?* At the top on the left.
> *Where's the milk bottle?* At the bottom on the left.

Exercise C

Give an example. You could use a milk bottle for a flower. Show on the board.

Set for pairwork. Monitor. Feed back, getting students to tell the class about the most imaginative uses.

Methodology note

This fun activity emphasizes the fact that *a liquid container* is empty, therefore you can use it for something else.

Exercise D

Remind students of the word *researcher*.

1 Set for individual work and pairwork checking. Play the tape. Give students plenty of time to work out the two types of questions. Monitor and assist, but do not feed back.
2 Set for pairwork. Monitor and assist, but do not feed back.
3 Refer students to Skills Check 3.

Feed back. Get the two kinds of sentence on the board as follows:

How much	*water*				
How many	*glasses of water*	*do*	*you*	*drink*	*every day?*

Point out that *water* is uncountable, but *glass* is countable.

Drill the *much/many* distinction and the relationship between containers and liquids as follows:

You say:	*water*
Students say:	*How much water?*
You say:	*glasses*
Students say:	*How many glasses of water?*
You say:	*milk*
Students say:	*How much milk?*, etc.

You say:	*milk*
Students say:	*How many glasses of milk?*
You say:	*coffee*
Students say:	*How many cups of coffee?*, etc.

Tapescript

Presenter:	Lesson 3
	D 1 Listen. She asks two kinds of questions. What are they?
Researcher:	Can I ask you some questions about your drinking habits?
Subject:	Yes, of course.
Researcher:	How much water do you drink every day?
Subject:	Mmm. Well, I know you should drink eight to ten glasses, but I don't. I probably drink two or three.
Researcher:	Thank you. And how many cans of cola or soft drinks?
Subject:	None. I hate sugary drinks.
Researcher:	Fine. What about milk? How much milk do you drink?
Subject:	None, oh, well, no. I drink milk in coffee and tea.
Researcher:	How much coffee do you drink every day?
Subject:	Oh, I love coffee. I drink far too much. Perhaps ten cups.
Researcher:	How many cups?!
Subject:	Ten, or perhaps twelve!

Exercise E

Set for pairwork. Monitor and assist. Tell students that the use of a tally chart is the best way to record this kind of research. If there is time, get students to turn the results into a bar chart.

Methodology note

Students should do this activity with a good standard of accuracy in construction and pronunciation.

Closure

Feed back on Exercise E, getting students to tell you about their partner.

Lesson 4: Speaking

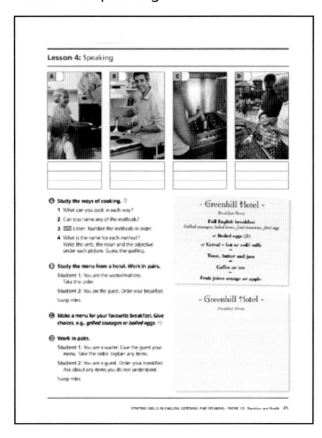

Introduction

1   If possible, take in a number of menus from different local restaurants. Hand them round and get students to try to identify items on each menu.
2   Mime different kinds of food and drink for students to identify – the sillier the better!
3   Ask students to do some mimes of food and drink items.

Exercise A

1   Refer students to the pictures. Elicit items for each method of cooking. Try not to say the method at this stage. Use *The first way, the second way*, etc., e.g., *You can cook cakes the first way.*
2   Set for pairwork. Do not confirm or correct.
3   Set for individual work and pairwork checking. Play the tape. Feed back, checking that students have correctly identified each method.

4   Set for pairwork. Feed back, getting the words on the board and checking the spelling.

Answers

3   C 1 boil
    B 2 fry
    D 3 grill
    A 4 bake

4

A	B	C	D
bake	fry	boil	grill
baking	frying	boiling	grilling
baked	fried	boiled	grilled

Methodology note

This is not really an exercise in teaching new words. Rather it is revision of the skill of guessing spelling from common patterns of sound-sight. These words conform to common sound-sight relationships, so students should not have great difficulty working out the spelling. If necessary, suggest similar known words for them to copy, e.g.,

bake = take
fry = cry, try
boil = oil, coin This is the hardest. Students may not know a similar word.
grill = ill, fill

Nouns and adjectives follow spelling patterns which students have learnt.

Tapescript

Presenter: Lesson 4
A 3 Listen. Number the methods in order.

Voice: There are four main ways to cook food. Firstly, we can put the food in water and boil the water. That means heat the water to one hundred degrees centigrade. So we can have boiled eggs, for example, or boiled potatoes. We can also boil vegetables.

We can put the food in butter or fat and heat it. This is called frying. We can have fried eggs or fried fish. We can fry some kinds of meat, too.

The third way is called grilling. We put the food under or over the heat. We don't need water or butter for grilling. We can grill fish or meat. We can also grill vegetables.

Finally, there is baking. We put the food inside an oven and heat it. We can bake potatoes or meat or fish. We can also bake cakes and biscuits.

Closure

Get some of the best pairs to demonstrate in front of the class.

Exercise B

Refer students to the menu. You may have to explain *sausages*, *beans* and *toast*. Set up the role play carefully. Monitor and assist. Feed back by asking the waiters in each case what the guests ordered. Swap roles.

Exercise C

Point out that students can write anything, in their own language, on the menu blank. But they must give one choice for the main meal. Monitor and assist. Ask a good student what is on his/her menu. Ask for an explanation. Demonstrate how you can explain a strange food, e.g.,
It's a kind of meat. It's grilled.
They are boiled vegetables.

Exercise D

Set up the pairwork. Monitor and assist. Ask students to swap roles.

THEME 1
Education

dictionary *(n)*

explain *(v)*

History *(n)*

learn *(v)*

Mathematics *(n)*

Science *(n)*

spell *(v)*

study *(v)*

teach *(v)*

university *(n)*

THEME 2
Daily Life

autumn *(n)*

late *(adj)*

later *(adj)*

midnight *(n)*

minute *(n)*

noon *(n)*

o'clock *(adv)*

past *(adv and n)*

quarter *(n)*

spring *(n)*

summer *(n)*

tomorrow *(n)*

tonight *(n)*

winter *(n)*

yesterday *(n)*

THEME 3
Work and Business

company *(n)*

e-mail *(n)*

envelope *(n)*

file *(n)*

letter *(n)*

manager *(n)*

shelf *(n)*

supermarket *(n)*

website *(n)*

working hours *(n)*

THEME 4
Science and Nature

flower *(n)*

fog *(n)*

forest *(n)*

rain *(n and v)*

river *(n)*

sea *(n)*

temperature *(n)*

thunderstorm *(n)*

water *(n)*

weather *(n)*

wind *(n)*

THEME 5
The Physical World

above *(prep)*

behind *(prep)*

below *(prep)*

between *(prep)*

corner *(n)*

in front of *(prep)*

in the centre of *(prep)*

near *(prep)*

next to *(prep)*

opposite *(prep)*

out (of an area) *(prep)*

THEME 6
Culture and Civilization

age *(n)*

born *(adj)*

congratulations *(n)*

dead *(adj)*

die *(v)*

family *(n)*

group *(n)*

guest *(n)*

married *(adj)*

party *(n)*

present *(n)*

single *(adj)*

thank *(v)*

thank you

THEME 7
They Made Our World

accident *(n)*

airport *(n)*

arrive *(v)*

bus stop *(n)*

driver *(n)*

land *(v)*

leave *(v)*

passenger *(n)*

pilot *(n)*

sailor *(n)*

street *(n)*

take off *(v)*

traffic *(n)*

THEME 8
Art and Literature

bring *(v)*

build *(v)*

carry *(v)*

check *(v)*

climb *(v)*

draw *(v)*

feel *(v)*

find *(v)*

live *(v)*

look *(v)*

make *(v)*

point *(v)*

put *(v)*

run *(v)*

say *(v)*

talk *(v)*

tell *(v)*

Word Lists: Thematic

THEME 9
Sports and Leisure

film (v)

hobby (n)

magazine (n)

news (n)

newspaper (n)

opera (n)

programme (n)

show (n)

sports (n)

turn off (v)

turn on (v)

THEME 10
Nutrition and Health

bottle (n)

breakfast (n)

cup (n)

dentist (n)

glass (n)

jam (n)

meal (n)

menu (n)

restaurant (n)

salt (n)

Word Lists: Alphabetical

above (prep)

accident (n)

age (n)

airport (n)

arrive (v)

autumn (n)

behind (prep)

below (prep)

between (prep)

born (adj)

bottle (n)

breakfast (n)

bring (v)

build (v)

bus stop (n)

carry (v)

check (v)

climb (v)

company (n)

congratulations (n)

corner (n)

cup (n)

dead (adj)

dentist (n)

dictionary (n)

die (v)

draw (v)

driver (n)

e-mail (n)

envelope (n)

explain (v)

family (n)

feel (v)

file (n)

film (v)

find (v)

flower (n)

fog (n)

forest (n)

glass (n)

group (n)

guest (n)

History (n)

hobby (n)

in front of (prep)

in the centre of (prep)

jam (n)

land (v)

late (adj)

later (adj)

learn (v)

leave (v)

letter (n)

live *(v)*

look *(v)*

magazine *(n)*

make *(v)*

manager *(n)*

married *(adj)*

Mathematics *(n)*

meal *(n)*

menu *(n)*

midnight *(n)*

minute *(n)*

near *(prep)*

news *(n)*

newspaper *(n)*

next to *(prep)*

noon *(n)*

o'clock *(adv)*

opera *(n)*

opposite *(prep)*

out (of an area) *(prep)*

party *(n)*

passenger *(n)*

past *(adv and n)*

pilot *(n)*

point *(v)*

present *(n)*

programme *(n)*

put *(v)*

quarter *(n)*

rain *(n and v)*

restaurant *(n)*

river *(n)*

run *(v)*

sailor *(n)*

salt *(n)*

say *(v)*

Science *(n)*

sea *(n)*

shelf *(n)*

show *(n)*

single *(adj)*

spell *(v)*

sports *(n)*

spring *(n)*

street *(n)*

study *(v)*

summer *(n)*

supermarket *(n)*

take off *(v)*

talk *(v)*

teach *(v)*

tell *(v)*

temperature *(n)*

thank *(v)*

thank you

thunderstorm *(n)*

tomorrow *(n)*

tonight *(n)*

traffic *(n)*

turn off *(v)*

turn on *(v)*

university *(n)*

water *(n)*

weather *(n)*

website *(n)*

wind *(n)*

winter *(n)*

working hours *(n)*

yesterday *(n)*